Léonie Caldecott was born in London and educated at the French Lycée and Oxford. In her early years as a freelance journalist she won the 1982 Catherine Pakenham Award. Since becoming a Roman Catholic, she has lectured on faith and culture in many places including Oxford Brookes and the Pontifical Council for Culture in Rome. She is associate director of the Thomas More Center for Faith and Culture in Oxford, where she lives with her husband and three daughters.

The cover image: the chalice and rosary beads capture two vital aspects of the Catholic faith. The rosary helps us meditate on the life of Christ as seen through the eyes of his first disciple: his mother, who gave him his human identity. The chalice – depicted in medieval times as the Holy Grail – contains the 'precious blood' shed for our salvation and bestowing true kinship with Christ.

SERIES EDITOR: TONY MORRIS

What Do **CATHOLICS** Believe?

Léonie Caldecott

Granta Books
London

Granta Publications, 12 Addison Avenue, London W11 4QR

First published in Great Britain by Granta Books 2008

A CIP catalogue record for this book is available
from the British Library.

1 3 5 7 9 10 8 6 4 2

ISBN 978-1-84708-003-5

Typeset by M Rules
Printed and bound in Great Britain by
J. H. Haynes & Co. Ltd., Sparkford

For my father, who first taught me to pray

I am all at once what Christ is, since he was what I am, and
This Jack, joke, poor potsherd, patch, matchwood, immortal diamond,
Is immortal diamond.

Gerard Manley Hopkins

Contents

Acknowledgements

I would like to thank a number of people who helped me in various ways, through prayer, practical help or constructive criticism, as I wrote this book. First and foremost is my husband, Stratford, without whom I would not have managed to bring this project to fruition at all. Thanks are also due to Tony Morris who entrusted the project to me, and Bella Shand, for her refining editorial hand in the last stages. I would also like to thank, in no particular order, for help both practical and spiritual, Sr Ann Catherine OP, Sr Jane Dominic OP, Adrian Walker, Brigitte and Jonathan and family, Fr Dominic. Finally credit goes to my daughters, Tessa, Sophie and Rosie, whose culinary skills and readiness for lively discussion around the dinner table enhanced the time of my labour. Plaudits for all errors and infelicities that remain go to me.

31 May 2007
Feast of the Visitation

Introduction

A Christian perspective

From the chilly autumnal night, I step into the softly lit cathedral. I move up a side aisle, towards the statue of the Virgin Mary. Mass is drawing to a close and all around me the congregation is gathering into queues, getting ready to receive communion. The church is very full. It is the feast of Our Lady of Walsingham. I fall to my knees in front of the medieval image of the Mother of God, a gift to this nineteenth-century Catholic cathedral from the far more venerable Westminster Abbey.

I am not there to receive communion – I have not attended the Mass. Yet my prayer in front of Mary takes on a particular quality: a quality that derives from the present focus of this large body of people. With a startling concreteness, Mary becomes present to me precisely as the human body which first contained that divine body, the body of her Son. Mary is the person who, more than any other, is mystically linked to the extraordinary story of God made man. An omnipotent God who elects to be born as a tiny, vulnerable baby from her womb – living among men, suffering and dying among men.

Here, at the culmination of the Mass, is the reality for which all Roman Catholics live: the sharing in that humanity of God incarnate, the participation – through an act as simple as eating – in his divinity. It is the feeding of the five thousand. It is the hordes of hungry souls down the sweep of history. I feel those souls in the souls around me, I am bound up with them. I understand myself as part of the body that is the Church, a body that finds its archetype in Mary, daughter of Zion, who first gave flesh to this paradoxical God whom we long to receive, not just as an abstract idea, but physically, intimately – on the tongue.

Twenty-two years before this I was also in a great cathedral. I was puzzling over the question of faith. My eye was drawn to a sumptuously coloured mural of Christ in glory, sitting in the midst of a mandorla, that opening created by the precise geometry where two circles intersect at each other's centre. It was the beauty that was holding my attention, yet this attention was not of an intellectual nature. My mind was in a spin, trying to come to grips with a double bind. On one side there were my doubts and fears about the Roman Catholic Church: issues to do with authority, dogma, freedom of conscience; fears about terrifying historical associations, crusades, heresy hunters, Borgia popes. Questions about the cult of saints, and in particular the Virgin Mary, who seemed to me so far removed from the rest of women as to be entirely inaccessible.

  Yet I could not tear myself away, on account of one thing: that tiny host, that wafer of bread, which Catholics receive at the end of Mass when they go to communion, believing that it has become the Body of Christ; not symbolically, metaphorically, but literally. At a particular moment in the Mass, called the consecration, Catholics believe this piece of wafer-thin bread becomes Christ himself. 'Take this and eat it, this is my body which will be given up for you,' he said at the Last Supper. 'Do this in memory of me.'

This is the heart of the matter: it is for this that I became a Catholic. In spite of my confusion, I knew I had to receive communion in order to be fed. It was that simple. The word Eucharist, which expresses this transformation of simple matter into the self and substance of God, is derived from the Greek word for thanksgiving. In the end it was my thanksgiving for what I received that motivated me to try to understand the context of the gift, just as you do with an incredibly thoughtful birthday present, which expresses perfectly the love that the giver has for you.

It never ceases to amaze me that in the modern, secularized world people are still fascinated by religion, in spite of attacks made on it by critics such as Richard Dawkins. Religion is a way of seeing, of being, of perceiving reality. Images can sum this up for us, striking through our ordinary life to some deeper level: an exultant goddess in a richly decorated Hindu painting; Jews at the Wailing Wall, rocking to and fro as they repeat the beautiful phrases of the Hebrew Scriptures; the beatific face of the Bodhisattva as he sits in meditation, a giant statue adorning a cliff-face in a remote part of Asia; the compelling eyes of the Mother of God in a Russian Orthodox church, her child encircling her neck with his hand as she looks across at you through a sea of candles and the deep harmonies of the eastern liturgy; the sight of Muslims at prayer in the dappled light of a mosque, all inclined towards the same focal point, unshod and abandoned to their devotion; Sufis turning as their robes billow out to make that perfect circle round the still point, which every heart yearns after.

Our desire to be in communion with something beyond

ourselves – the experience of that mysterious contact – is found in testimonies from every culture and time. 'Mysterious' does not mean 'irrational': reason plays a considerable role in the belief system you will read about in this book. For Catholics, reason is essential in unpacking faith. But without the *content* of faith, the lived encounter with that Other, which lies at the heart of our religious practice, reason would be redundant, a machine snapping at empty air.

We have to make use of both faith and reason in explaining what Catholics believe. These are two sides of the same coin: complementary aspects of human experience, right-brain function in precisely calibrated balance with left-brain function. On the one hand there is the voice that adumbrates the structure, the rational belief system, which gives us access to the faith; then there is the voice that speaks of the heart, the lived experience of that faith. In recent years there have been moves in theological circles to bring theology, as an intellectual reflection on faith and Scripture, back into contact with spirituality again. This has been called *doing theology on your knees*. It's about time.

There is a statue that stands over the door of my parish church, a statue of Jesus as the Good Shepherd. He stands there, watching people go in and out. His face wears a smile, his body stands in a relaxed position, hoisting a lamb on his shoulders. With his right hand he holds the lamb's feet to keep it steady. With his left hand he grasps a shepherd's crook. But it is the expression on the face of the lamb that fascinates me most. The lamb has no intention of falling off those shoulders: he is pressed against that neck as though he were aspiring to become a part of it. His face is blissful. He looks down at you just as the Shepherd does. And that's the point: he's in the perfect position to see everything from the point of view of the person who carries him up there on his shoulders. He has perspective.

For me, this image expresses something crucial about Christianity. At its heart is something that goes beyond doctrinal arguments or moral conundrums. It is an invitation not simply to believe in Christ, but to be lifted up to his level, to try to share his perspective on ourselves and those around us. This is an interior thing, of course, and we don't manage it most of the time. But Christianity is void and useless without this possibility, since it is this close relationship with the God made man which makes us more than just Sunday pew fillers. The Christian religion is first and foremost about relationship, beginning with the relationship between God and man.

The first place we have to look to understand this relationship is sacred Scripture. One of the most famous of the Jewish Scriptures, found in what Christians call the Old Testament, is the book of Genesis, which recounts the creation of the world. Catholics think of such texts as symbolic in style – even in the fourth century St Augustine knew that the world was not created in seven days, as we think of time. This does not mean that these Scriptures are not profoundly true. Written under the influence of divine inspiration, they were intended to explain not the science of creation but its meaning for us and our relationship with God. Thus the creation is shown as having a sevenfold structure, ending with a day set aside for prayer.

Later in Genesis God promises to bless Abraham's descendants and make them more numerous than the stars. Through that relationship (which the Bible calls a 'covenant'), and the inspiration that God gave to the prophets and authors of the Bible who descended from Abraham, the divine nature was revealed in a special way. God was more than just a tribal deity. He was God of the whole universe and the maker of all that is, but at the same time he was a God who wanted to be with his people, in their very midst.

To be understood, God's decision has to be set against the background of the Fall, described in the third chapter of Genesis. There we find the aboriginal story of mankind's first parents, Adam and Eve. They disobeyed God's order that they should not eat the fruit of a certain tree in the garden of Eden – 'the tree of the knowledge of good and evil'. Eve gave in to the temptation of the serpent, who told her that if she and her husband tasted the fruit they would 'become as gods'. She plucked and ate the fruit, and persuaded Adam to do the same. This abuse of human freedom (for God is portrayed as commanding but not compelling) is called Original Sin. It resulted in the Fall, that is to say a breakdown in communion between man and God, and mankind's expulsion from Eden. The rest of the Old Testament relates how God tried to repair the breach through one particular people, the Israelites, descendants of Abraham.

The Christian New Testament goes one step further. It shows God taking the covenant that he had made with the Jewish people and opening it up to everyone, creating a universal religion. He does this in an unprecedented way, not simply by speaking through another prophet, but by taking on human nature – a body and soul like ours – in order to reveal himself as fully as possible to us in a language we can all understand, whatever race or tribe we belong to. 'For as by a man came death, by a man has come also the resurrection of the dead. For as in Adam all die, so also in Christ shall all be made alive' (1 Corinthians 15:21–2). Christians believe that God effectively sent a 'second Adam' to redeem the fault of the first one: he sent his own son, Jesus Christ. The life of Christ is recorded in the Gospels, four documents written after Jesus's death and forming the core Scripture of Christianity.

Jesus was crucified by the Romans at the instigation of the Jewish authorities, essentially for blasphemy (that is, for implying or claiming that he was equal to God). He voluntarily accepted this terrible death as a way of taking on himself the consequences of human alienation from God. But he rose from the dead and ascended into heaven, proving that death no longer had any power over him, and promised eternal life to anyone who would join him- or herself to him in faith, hope and love.

Christians believe that what Jesus reveals to us is both man and God. He reveals the nature of God as love. The central message of the Gospels is that only in loving God and each other can we find our own ultimate fulfilment and meaning. This characterizes the way prayer is experienced by the Christian. It is the God who lifts us up on his shoulders who makes us capable of prayer. And 'prayer' does not refer only to verbal communication. Perhaps the simplest definition is 'turning the mind and the heart towards God': a kind of pure attentiveness. For a Christian, prayer is the joint work of God and the human being, for our spiritual or interior life depends on a profound cooperation with God. On our own we can question and praise and ask, but only the presence of God makes these interior actions into a real communication with him, which gives us the possibility of seeing things from a divine perspective.

1

The quality of mercy: seven sacraments

> The quality of mercy is not strained,
> It droppeth as the gentle rain from heaven
> Upon the place beneath.
>
> *The Merchant of Venice*

The life of the Catholic Church revolves around what we call the *sacraments* (a word that originally meant simply 'mysteries'). The celebration and reception of these 'visible signs of invisible grace' make God's presence manifest in spite of man's inadequacy. Grace simply means the divine gift that enables us to 'breathe' spiritually with God in our everyday lives. In an ideal world those who received these gifts would manifest the graceful, unstrained quality that they embody all the time. But fallen human nature loves a struggle and only periodically surrenders to the quality of mercy that God is ready to pour out for it.

There are seven sacraments in the Catholic Church: Baptism, Confirmation, Marriage, Ordination (or Priesthood), Reconciliation (also known as Confession or Penance), Eucharist and the Anointing of the Sick (which used to be called Extreme Unction).

Baptism, Confirmation and Anointing

Not every Christian Church baptizes babies as well as adults, but the Catholic Church has done so from the earliest times, when whole households were received into the Church together. Baptism was a rite of spiritual cleansing, foreshadowed by Jesus's baptism in the River Jordan at the hands of his cousin John, known as 'the Baptist'. From a Christian point of view John the Baptist was the last prophet of the Old Covenant, calling on the Jewish people to repent of their hypocrisy, as many prophets had done, and to mark this desire for reconciliation with God by immersion in the purifying waters of the Jordan. To the Baptist, a voice 'crying out in the wilderness' (Matthew 3:3) for man to prepare the way for God, water was the obvious medium to express the abundance of life that only God can give, like the clean waters gushing from under the temple in the vision of the Prophet Ezekiel, a Jewish prophet from around six hundred years earlier. Later, when Jesus told his followers to baptize 'in the name of the Father and of the Son and of the Holy Spirit' (Matthew 28:19), Baptism became a Christian sacrament of initiation, making the baptized person a member of Christ's Church.

The angel brought me to the entrance of the Temple, where a stream came out from under the Temple threshold and flowed eastwards, since the Temple faced east. The water flowed from under the right side of the Temple, south of the altar … He said, This water flows east down to the Arabah and to the sea; and flowing into the sea it makes its waters wholesome. Wherever the river flows, all living creatures teeming in it will live. Fish will be very plentiful, for wherever the water goes it brings health, and life teems wherever the river flows. Along the river, on either bank, will grow every kind of fruit tree with leaves that never wither and fruit that never fails; they will bear new fruit every month, because this water comes from the sanctuary. And their fruit will be good to eat and the leaves medicinal.

Ezekiel 47:1–12 (cf. Revelation 22:1–2)

Often we talk about the waters of baptism (now normally given from a font in the church, not from a river in the open air) as 'washing away sins'. You may ask, why on earth would a baby *need* to be cleansed of sin? Surely he or she has done nothing yet which could need to be forgiven or washed away? You would be right, if you were thinking of that small person in isolation from his or her biological and spiritual roots, or the other parts of life still to come. But a sacrament is something that comes into time from *out of time*, a sign in the here and now of a greater timeless reality, which is coming into contact with the life of that child. A child is baptized to heal the inherited fault line that comes down from original sin. The child's parents invite godparents, whose role begins by making the baptismal promises on behalf of the child, and by undertaking to help it live out this God-given grace through the rest of its life.

The water also represents the place in which we intend the child to live: in the life-giving water that flows out from the temple, to hark back to that powerful vision of Ezekiel's. In baptism a person is adopted by God, becomes a child of God *in and through Christ.* For Catholics the temple seen in the vision of Ezekiel is a foreshadowing of Christ. On many occasions in the Gospels Jesus refers to the connection between himself and the prophecies of the Old Testament. At the end of his life, when he has arrived in Jerusalem before his passion and death, he directly refers to himself as the temple: knock it down, he says, and in three days it will be rebuilt (John 2:19–22). Not until after his resurrection, which occurred on the third day after his death, was this imagery understood by his followers.

The practice of infant baptism underlines one crucial aspect of all the sacraments of initiation (that is, Baptism, Confirmation and Eucharist). This is the fact that they are not merely subjective in nature, but objective. You don't have to understand fully, or indeed be fully worthy of what you are receiving, in order to receive it. Sacraments are free gifts from God, given through the Church. It is tempting to think of confirmation as a sort of 'rite of passage' for teenagers, who when confirmed will assume for themselves the responsibility for declaring and practising their faith, when in fact the grace of confirmation operates on a supernatural level that goes beyond any conscious determination on the part of the person receiving it.

And yet the idea of confirmation as marking the threshold of mature faith is not entirely false. Confirmation should mark an important moment in the life of young persons, a period in which they begin to think for themselves about the gift of membership in the Church that was given them in baptism. Originally confirmation was given immediately after adult baptism, and even today it is the sacrament given to Christians wishing to enter the Catholic Church who have already been baptized elsewhere (their baptism does not have to be repeated because the Catholic Church recognizes the validity of Christian baptism no matter in which denomination it was received).

Confirmation is usually conferred by the bishop, as the representative of the universal Church, who, as he lays his hands on the confirmand's head, stands for an unbroken line of apostles who have laid their hands on the faithful and prayed for them to receive the Holy Spirit. A person who has been confirmed is supposed to receive seven very specific 'gifts of the Spirit' (see Isaiah 11:2–3). These are called Wisdom, Counsel, Knowledge, Understanding, Fortitude, Piety and Wonder/Awe of the Lord. These spiritual gifts are given in confirmation; and if they are not immediately apparent in the behaviour and personality of the person who has just been confirmed, we have to remind ourselves that whether we open the gift, continue to appreciate it fully, let alone use it well, is up to us.

The gifts of the Holy Spirit should lead to twelve 'fruits' or results in the individual. Jesus used the image of fruiting trees extensively in his parables. For example, he said that false prophets would be 'known by their fruits' (Matthew 7:16) and another time spoke of a gardener who found no fruit on his tree after three years and was persuaded to give it one more chance – just as God gives us one more chance to bear fruit in our own lives (Luke 13:6–9). The fruits of the Spirit's work in an individual are Charity, Joy, Peace, Patience, Kindness, Goodness, Generosity, Gentleness, Faithfulness, Modesty, Self-control and Chastity (see St Paul's Letter to the Galatians 5:22–3).

There is what Catholics call a 'royal priesthood', the priesthood not just of ministers but of all the people, who have been adopted into union with Christ and hence into being sons or daughters of the Father. Once again, it is up to us whether we allow the fruits of this adoption to grow and ripen in us. A Christian is supposed to receive these gifts actively, not passively. We are supposed to ask for them over and over again, not just at confirmation, but all through our lives.

A sacrament, then, is not something that depends on, or even is necessarily manifested by, the recipient; it is not some mood-enhancing magic, or quantifiable ability to be good:

rather it is what Catholics call a 'grace'. A grace is something we receive from God, a gift whose sole purpose is to draw us closer to him and make us ready to be one with him now and after death: that is to say, to live with him for ever in heaven. The 'now' part of that equation is as important as the 'after' part. Catholics are given the means to sacramentalize every part of their daily existence, that is to allow God to manifest himself through that earthly existence. This is why many Catholics do not only go to church on Sundays, but try to attend Mass every day.

The same objective reality applies to the Anointing of the Sick, which is often given by a priest when the sick person is too weak to move, or to cooperate outwardly with the sacrament. All that is required is some indication that the person is willing to receive it, or would have been willing if conscious. It marks his or her preparedness to be healed of personal sin (that is to say of all the choices they have made that separate them from the divine life), something in which the body plays a major role, being the executor of the human will. And so the priest anoints the body with holy oil; oil is also used at baptism and confirmation. By entering definitively into the divine life and leaving behind earthly existence, the seriously ill or dying person marks a new phase in his or her development towards eternal life.

The Spousal Mystery (Marriage)

Confirmation, Eucharist and most of the other sacraments require a priest because the priesthood was instituted precisely to make these sacraments possible. The sacrament of marriage, however, is sometimes called the 'primordial' sacrament, because a form of it dates back to the very earliest times, before there was a Christian priesthood. The freely self-giving love of man and woman comes from the mind and heart of God in the beginning; but with the coming of Christ, the union of man and woman has been able to participate more fully in the Trinitarian life of God as an image of his sacrifice and as a source of grace. It is fitting, then, that the minister of the sacrament is not the priest. The couple administer the sacrament to each other, with the priest acting as witness on behalf of the Church.

The goal of marriage as understood by a Catholic Christian is not only to have children, but also for each spouse to help the other get to heaven. Having children, making a home and everything else involved in a marriage are all part of that fundamental pattern: we are opened up to the divine life, to heaven, if we share our lives with others. Just as raw stones become smooth and polished as they come into contact with one another, human souls develop in an extraordinary way by the close contact with one another that is family life. The most important thing in a marriage, from the Catholic point of view, is its fruit: children are the most obvious type of fruitfulness, but they are not the only one. You could say the first child of a marriage is the 'couple' itself – meaning a shared life that is more than the sum of its parts.

Catholic teaching on marriage is highly controversial in our day, but in fact it is not possible to understand it unless you understand that for Catholics it reflects the Trinity in heaven, and the union of divinity and humanity in Christ. This is the mystery of which St Paul speaks in his Letter to the Ephesians (5:21–33), a passage that has attracted misogynist abuse, and more latterly feminist ire, against this persecutor of the early Church (then known as Saul), whose dramatic conversion on the road to Damascus did not entirely strip the zealot out of the newly won apostle. 'The husband is the head of the wife just as Christ is the head of the Church, the body of which he is the Saviour' is a passage which certainly sits uncomfortably with us today.

What is usually ignored when this phrase is taken out of context, however, is that Paul has prefaced it with another piece of advice: 'Be *subject to one another* out of reverence for Christ.' Furthermore, while he enjoins wives to be 'subject' to their husbands, he spends much more time enjoining husbands to love their wives as Christ loved the Church. Only a husband who is Christlike in his love would have the right to demand obedience, according to Paul – and of course the more Christlike he is the less he would want to assert it (read Mark 10:42–5, 'the Son of Man came not to be served but to serve', and also John 13:12–17). In general it is unhelpful to cite Scripture out of context, which is why Catholics try to read Scripture holistically as part of a long tradition, beginning with the Church fathers, of reflection on the deeper meaning of Scripture.

St Paul's central thought taken in context, therefore, is not as misogynistic as it first appears. Jesus's teaching actually transformed the meaning of 'subjection', just as he radically transformed the meaning of 'love' by showing us in his own life and death what it could mean. This most intimate relation between women and men 'is a great mystery, and I mean in reference to Christ and his Church', says Paul. The sacrament of marriage is a privileged participation in the spousal union between Christ and the Church, with the Church here playing the role of Christ's bride. This nuptial theme finds its roots in the Old Testament imagery of God and his people Israel as joined like man and wife, so it is not surprising to find St Paul using his own religious heritage as a means of reflecting back on the human union.

Marriage taps right in to the central mystery of Christianity and for that reason Catholic marriage is in principle indissoluble. Obviously a mere legal contract can be dissolved with a stroke of the pen, but a sacrament is more than that; it is a mutual vow to love and serve until death, not just until one or other party decides to end the relationship. Nothing else, no other intention, could serve to meld two lives into one new life, one flesh, in the way that sacramental marriage does. Just as good parents accept their child in all its individuality, and not because the child gratifies or pleases them, so spouses learn to show mercy towards their other half. And by showing this kind of mercy, this deference before the incomprehensible mystery of the other, each spouse begins to be 'divinized' (made godlike) by participating in God's own mystery.

Nonetheless, the Church holds that sometimes there is a flaw in the intention of the couple or a circumstance which invalidates the sacrament from the very start, and that this may only become clear later on. That is the basis on which the Church permits 'annulment'. This is not just a Catholic version of divorce, but rather amounts to saying the marriage never became completely sacramental in the first place, no matter how much love and goodwill may have been present at the start. (Naturally, when wealth or celebrity appears to make it easier to obtain an annulment this practice can easily fall into disrepute, however firmly rooted it is in the theology of marriage.)

This is a good place to mention monks and nuns and the whole concept of 'consecrated virginity'. For Catholics this does not just refer to a person who has not (yet) had sexual intercourse, but to a deliberately chosen state of life that excludes sexual activity, yet is closely linked to the nuptial mystery of the Church. In this case the consecration signifies the spiritual espousal of Christ (for women) and of his Church (for men). In other words the supernatural love of Christ or the Church takes the place in a person's life normally reserved for the natural love of another human being in marriage.

Traditionally this state was embraced only by those who belonged to a religious order or community of monks, friars, nuns or sisters. Monasteries or 'monasticism' still have a central place in the Catholic Church, providing a powerhouse of constant, disciplined prayer, and in some cases apostolic service on a practical level, on which everyone depends. But in our day new forms of consecrated life in the lay state have come into being. Movements such as Focolare, the Neo-Catechumenal way or Communion and Liberation, communities such as Opus Dei, San Egidio or the Spiritual Family of the Work, where people elect to live together in order to support one another in their lives as Catholics, all contain people who have taken vows of one kind or another. Such people live in the world, often doing ordinary jobs, yet they live like the leaven hidden in the dough, the smallest amount of which can transform the whole. The central notion of consecration is to orientate one's life entirely to the service of Christ and his Church, in a conscious manner sealed by a vow.

Anointed for Life: the Sacrament of Orders (Priesthood)

When most people think of the Catholic Church, one of the first images that springs to mind is a priest with his 'dog collar' and vestments. This is not surprising, given the absolute centrality of the sacraments in the Catholic way of life. For without the priest, the sacraments could not be perpetuated. Priesthood goes back to the pre-Christian idea of a man set apart to offer sacrifice to the gods on behalf of the people. In the Old Testament, the priest-king Melchizedek offered a sacrifice of bread and wine rather than animals (Genesis 14:18), a foreshadowing, according to Catholics, of the sacrifice of the Mass. Christ offers on the Cross the one and only necessary sacrifice to the one God. But in order to bring that one sacrifice to everyone, some men are specially anointed to represent Christ in his role as priest.

So it is not surprising that the act of conferring the priesthood, or what is called the sacrament of 'Holy Orders', is taken so seriously. At one point during the ceremony of ordination the candidate lays himself flat on his face in front of the altar and remains there for what seems like an age, while the Litany of Saints is recited (*Saint A, pray for us. Saint B, pray for us. Saint C, pray for us.* And so on). There could be no more compelling way of expressing what he is about to do. He is literally laying his life down for God: handing himself over, offering all his days for the service of the people of God.

A man is standing in a momentous place when he presents himself for the sacrament of orders. He is getting ready to stand in for the Bridegroom, Christ, who comes to unite himself with his Bride, the Church. He must love the Bride with the same outpouring of self that the true Bridegroom shows on the Cross. Yet the fact that he expresses this through the most radical body language (prostration), precisely while the support and prayers of the saints is invoked, gives a vital clue to the context that will help him carry this out. It is in *communion*, in deep fellowship with his brothers and sisters, that he will be enabled to follow through with this vow. It is for this communion, this availability to all, that he is normally asked, in the Catholic Church, to remain celibate. There is a parallel moment for a woman who is taking solemn vows to become a nun, when she lays her hands between the hands of her superior, affirming with this body language her availability to the rest of the body of believers.

It is true that priests often fail to live up to what is demanded of them. From a purely human point of view the Catholic ideal of the priesthood is not an easy thing to maintain. This is why the calling of a man to this vocation is enshrined not just in a ceremony, but is one of the seven sacraments, that is to say in the continuation of Christ's own life in the world, among men and women. Paradoxically, ordination sets a man apart, even as it makes him available as a servant to all. Before his death on the cross, Jesus prays to his Father: 'They are not of the world, even as I am not of the world. Sanctify them in the truth; your word is truth. As you sent me into the world, so I have sent them into the world. And for their sake I consecrate myself, that they also may be consecrated in truth' (John 17:16–19).

If a priest draws on that supernatural source of grace, he will have the strength to live out his vocation. Otherwise, he may end up living a divided, fractured life. He may fall into clericalism: the desire to impose his will by force, or by subterfuge, shoring up his own status at the expense of the gospel he is sent to preach. This temptation to dominate is not disconnected from the scandals that have rocked the Church in recent times, caused by priests who so successfully compartmentalized their own interests from those of the most vulnerable members of their flocks that they completely lost sight of their true vocation. To use another person, especially a child, for self-gratification is totally contrary to the Christian ethos, let alone the solemn vows made at ordination. A priest has been asked to become a true father to all his flock, and sexual abuse is the furthest thing from a fatherly act, just as it would be for a biological father. The horror of this may explain why some bishops have been scandalously slow in taking this problem seriously. It is literally unthinkable for a man who truly cares about Christ, who is most particularly present in the smallest and weakest members of his body in the Church, to engage in such a betrayal of trust, and hard to suspect others of doing so.

But the abuse of power has other manifestations too. If a priest calculates his own advantage, if he is cynical and dismissive, if he gossips about his flock rather than looking at them through Christlike eyes, he is acting like a 'hired hand' (John 10:11–15), rather than like a true shepherd. Jesus warned that such people allow the wolf into the sheepfold. For the behaviour of a pastor, especially in a church where the priest plays such a central role at both a supernatural and natural level, has a knock-on effect among his parishioners. It is a leadership position like no other: full of responsibility, yet without worldly reward, and increasingly under attack, if only because of the appalling behaviour that forces good priests to suffer on account of their wayward brethren. A priest in our day may need to be something of a hero to stick it out.

Yet when a priest truly lives out the intentions of Christ, no matter what his idiosyncrasies, he will radiate the love of God and be a sign of hope for all who encounter him. This can happen even when the priest doesn't feel strong enough to cope. In fact, the less proud he is of himself, the more grace flows through him. It is the opposite of a worldly career where self-assurance is the key. This is what a priest makes all those sacrifices for: so as to be a clear channel, an unencumbered light for others. Lay people can do many things in the Church, including tactfully and charitably supporting their pastors, but what they cannot do is administer those constant sources of grace, the forgiveness of sins and the Eucharist. For these the priest is specially empowered by Christ.

It is this connection with a God experienced both as Father and as Bridegroom that explains why the Catholic priesthood is reserved to men. The Catholic instinct seems to be that God uses the symbolism of gender as a vital element in the sacrament, just as he uses the symbolism of bread, wine, oil and water in other sacraments. The self-sacrifice of Christ on the Cross, which engenders the Church, is likened to the outpouring of self on the part of a man for his wife, as touched on in the previous section about the nuptial mystery.

The role of women in the Church is vital and it takes many forms: but not this one. Recent popes have ruled out the ordination of women once and for all, saying that the Catholic Church does not even have the *power* to ordain women. You need to have a deep understanding of both the priesthood (which, as I said before, is not a career) and of the central role that gender symbolism plays in the Catholic faith in order to understand this position. Pope John Paul II, who was a trained philosopher with a long-standing interest in the 'phenomenology' of human experience, and who also numbered many women among his close friends and associates, produced one of the most interesting documents on the role of women in the Church and the world: *Mulieris Dignitatem* (*On the Dignity of Women*, 1988). As well as inveighing against the exploitation of women in every sector from the workplace to the home, from war zones to the city streets, John Paul II analysed the meaning of spiritual maternity and its crucial contribution to the good of society. Far from defining women by the biological capacity to bear children, he turned the equation on its head by making the capacity to create a different kind of ethos from the male-dominated one an essential contribution both in the Church and outside it. It is not just a matter of becoming a biological mother. Physical maternity must participate in this reality, but so must every other sector in which women are, quite rightly, centrally involved.

There is no space to go into this document in detail here, but suffice it to say that it is very far from being a tokenist nod in the direction of 'the ladies, God bless them …'. In fact, the pressure for the ordination of women is, I suspect, stoked by the inability of many churchmen fully to acknowledge in their hearts the particular contribution women are capable of making. Both John Paul II and his successor, Benedict XVI, have ensured that women are employed in as many capacities as possible, for example, as theologians and administrators, and have stated their concern that a deeper understanding of the role of women should be developed by the Church.

Getting back to the issue of the priesthood, it is worth noting that in Catholic theology and spirituality there is an interesting parallel between the total involvement in the experience of motherhood for a woman and the fatherly pouring out of self in a man who becomes a priest. Neither vocation fits into a materialist, aspirational, goal-orientated idea of human society. Both vocations involve a fair amount of suffering – which is taken on board only because it is profoundly fruitful. Certainly, if a priest does not know how to be a spiritual father, he has missed out on the most crucial aspect of his vocation.

It is from among the ranks of priests that bishops, archbishops, cardinals and ultimately the pope, are chosen. I will talk more about these offices in the structure of the Church in chapter 3.

Eucatastrophe I: the Sacrament of Reconciliation (Confession)

Jesus Christ died on the Cross and was buried in a tomb, which was immediately sealed and guarded by Roman soldiers. On the third day after this happened (on the second day, it being the Jewish Sabbath, no one could go to the tomb) he appeared to one of his women followers, Mary Magdalene, who had gone with other women to the tomb, intending to anoint his body. He told her to go to Peter and the other Apostles and tell them he was resurrected from the dead; interestingly the men did not at first believe the women (Luke 24:11). Peter and John then went to the tomb and found that indeed the body was gone. However, none of the men actually saw the resurrected Christ in person until he appeared to them as a group in a house where they were hiding. The first thing he told them was that they should become vessels of his mercy to others: formally releasing others, in his name, from their sins.

In the evening of that same day, the first day of the week, the doors were closed in the room where the disciples were, for fear of the Jews. Jesus came and stood among them. He said to them, 'Peace be with you,' and showed them his hands and his side. The disciples were filled with joy when they saw the Lord, and he said to them again, 'Peace be with you. As the Father sent me, so I am sending you.' After saying this he breathed on them again and said: 'Receive the Holy Spirit. For those whose sins you forgive, they are forgiven; for those whose sins you retain, they are retained.'

John 20:19–23

When I became a Catholic at the age of twenty-seven, I was pet-rified of going to confession. To have to go and tell a priest all my mistakes, my failings, my *stuff* – what an appalling idea! I spent the morning before the dreaded event exploring the church of San Clemente in Rome. There are many layers to this church, from the Early Renaissance upper level to the more primitive church underneath, with extraordinary wall paint-ings that evoke the simple and eloquent spirit of the early Christian community, to a truly subterranean layer that used to be a pre-Christian Mithraic temple, through which one of Rome's underground rivers flows. As the waters rushed by me in the darkness, I knew that I would have to plunge into the inte-rior version of this freezing stygian torrent if I was to proceed on my journey towards the Church. Confession, or the sacrament of penance, can be like the cold shock of self-examination we all sometimes go through in the early hours of the morning when we remember some mistake made the previous day and think, 'Why the hell did I do that?'

Another name for this sacrament, however, is the sacrament of reconciliation. It is not meant to be a terrifying thing, which leaves us at the mercy of our self-doubt or the unsympathetic perspective of another person who is angry with us. The priest who hears a confession is there only on behalf of Christ, to dis-pense divine forgiveness and to enable the penitent to start afresh. During his lifetime Jesus frequently offered forgiveness to people whom the rest of society was inclined to despise or fear. If the Catholic faith means anything, it means that a person is not defined by his or her past mistakes. Also, the mystery at the heart of this sacrament can only be grasped in relation to a holistic view of where we fit in an imperfect world.

A question frequently posed to all who believe in God, and

Christians in particular, is how a good and all-powerful God can allow so much evil to happen in the world. This is a question to which only the appalling sight of Jesus hanging on the ultimate instrument of torture can provide an answer. And that answer is not a neat and tidy one. It is almost something of which one cannot speak, so gut-wrenching a solution is it. In brief, Christians believe that God sent his only begotten Son, not merely to live among us and share our human experience, but actually to go deep into the heart of the central problem of human existence, deep into the heart of darkness that lurks inside us all. So deep did he go that he actually vanquished evil itself, and the ultimate sign of evil's presence, namely death.

If you have experienced pain, whether the involuntary pain of loss or defeat, or the pain of contemplating your own failures and weakness, you know that taste of death. The experience of evil is the experience of annihilation, the assassination of something you hold dear, something you care about, something you know matters. What the passion and death of Christ accomplish is the breaking apart of that dark vortex of evil. There is an apt, if only partial, image for this mysterious dynamic of sacrifice taken to the extreme in the final part of the *Matrix* films. The hero allows the 'evil' programme to enter into him, consenting to die in order to stage a kind of counter-invasion of this legion of mocking, nihilistic faces.

These are simply images, with no specific Christian intent. But they point up the base-line intuition that even our post-Christian culture is drawn to when reflecting on the question of how ultimate evil can be confronted. J. R. R. Tolkien, the Catholic author of *The Lord of the Rings*, wrote about something he called the 'eucatastrophe', which is the moment in a story when tribulation and even seeming disaster are turned round, and good is drawn out of evil. This 'joyous turn', as

Tolkien calls it, would not be possible without the seeming triumph of evil coming first, the trials and tribulations, the catastrophe of power run amok.

Thus the first sin of mankind, whereby Adam and Eve sought power for its own sake by biting into the forbidden fruit and hid their faces from the God they were used to consorting with openly, is resolved in the Christian story as a *felix culpa*, a 'happy' or blessed fault (in the words of the Easter liturgy). For this aboriginal disaster, this fall from grace, would eventually serve as the basis for an even greater proof of God's love. Coming down to earth as one of us, sharing our condition and finally seeming utterly defeated in death, God in the person of Jesus Christ demonstrates that he can really go the distance with us. And so the *eu* (good, or happy) element, the divine spark that goes beyond our comprehension and elicits an amazed thankfulness, enters into the catastrophe and transforms it.

This is the mystery celebrated in the sacrament of 'reconciliation', or 'penance', where Catholics confess their sins in the hearing of a priest. It bears both names because it contains both aspects. We want to be reconciled with God, to be no longer alienated from him, and we ourselves need to go the distance to prove this. We do things, even small things, to prove we are sincere: this is called *doing penance*. For a Catholic, all the sacraments are acting out a mystery (the 'Paschal' or Easter mystery of death and resurrection), a visible sign of invisible grace. Jesus put his body on the line, so we put our bodies on the line too.

First, rather than simply saying sorry in our hearts, we go to a special place, engage in a simple ritual that places us intentionally in the presence of God and speak out loud in that privileged forum about our spiritual condition. Confession can take place anywhere, so long as it is private and out of the hearing of others. Usually people go into a special box in the church, where the penitent kneels on one side of a screen, and the priest sits on the other, facing sideways to the penitent so as to emphasize that he is only there *in persona Christi* (representing Christ). The confessor simply lends his ear to the process of scrutiny, which must come first and foremost from the conscience of the person confessing, even if the priest offers advice and support. There and under those circumstances alone, the priest has the authority delegated by Christ to absolve our sins. By putting ourselves in this position in relation to Christ, we are in effect letting ourselves be loved by him.

THE PARABLE OF THE PRODIGAL SON

Then Jesus said, 'There was a man who had two sons. The younger of them said to his father, "Father, give me the share of the property that will belong to me." So he divided his property between them. A few days later the younger son gathered all he had and travelled to a distant country, and there he squandered his property in dissolute living. When he had spent everything, a severe famine took place throughout that country, and he began to be in need. So he went and hired himself out to one of the citizens of that country, who sent him to his fields to feed the pigs. He would gladly have filled himself with the pods that the pigs were eating; and no one gave him anything. But when he came to himself he said, "How many of my father's hired hands have bread enough and to spare, but here I am dying of hunger! I will get up and go to my father, and I will say to him, 'Father, I have sinned against heaven and before you; I am no longer worthy to be called your son; treat me like one of your hired hands.'" So he set off and went to his father. But while he was still far off, his father saw him and was filled with compassion; he ran and put his arms around him and kissed him. Then the son said to him, "Father, I have sinned against heaven and before you; I am no longer worthy to be called your son." But the father said to his slaves, "Quickly, bring out a robe – the best one – and put it on him; put a ring on his finger and sandals on his feet. And get the fatted calf and kill it, and let us eat and celebrate; for this son of mine was dead and is alive again; he was lost and is found!"'

Luke 15:11

The penance that Catholics do after confession to demonstrate the joyous turn effected by God's forgiveness can consist of anything from saying specific prayers to reading a passage of Scripture, or to putting right some harm we have done to others. If we were to imagine this in the context of the story of the Prodigal Son, it might consist in the son doing something loving for his father – something that expressed his gratitude. In any case this particular sacrament is intensely personal and it is part of a long spiritual journey. Catholics don't believe that we are saved once and for all in this life – because our freedom to turn away from God continues till the moment of death – so they make regular use of this sacrament to progress spiritually and personally. God's grace works in each of us in a unique way, as unique as our fingerprints. The priest, acting only as a channel for God's grace, is strictly forbidden to reveal what is said in the confessional. What is spoken there remains a secret between the soul and God.

Eucatastrophe II: the Mass

We have come, at the end of this chapter, to the very heart of what Catholics believe. To a Catholic the Mass is the most important sacramental act of all. It is the reason priests are consecrated. Baptism and confirmation open the door to it, reconciliation prepares us for it, but the Mass is the nearest we come to heaven on earth, our final initiation into the Body of Christ.

The Mass is a complex and beautiful prayer in which priest and people, gathered before an altar or table of sacrifice, offer their thanks to God (it is also called the 'Eucharist', which means 'thanksgiving'). Because of its importance, all Catholics are obliged to go to Mass on Sundays and also on other major holy days during the year, known as 'holy days of obligation'. But a lot more than thanksgiving is going on in the Mass.

The ceremony begins with an act of repentance for any sins committed, known as the Penitential Rite. Then comes the Liturgy of the Word, which means a series of readings from Scripture – both the Old and New Testament, including one of the psalms. Next we come to the Eucharistic Rite, in which the people symbolically offer bread and wine (this is also when the collection plate is passed round for people to make a donation, if they can, for the support of the Church), and the priest takes these gifts and offers them to God. The bread and wine recall the ancient sacrifice of the mysterious priest Melchizedek I alluded to earlier. But because Jesus Christ is present in the priest by virtue of his ordination for this purpose, what happens next is a kind of miracle. The bread and wine become mysteriously identified with the sacrifice Christ made of his own life, at the Last Supper and on the Cross. In other words, they cease to be bread and wine any more, and become the body and blood of Christ. Finally, in the Communion Rite, the people go up to receive the body of Christ in a fragment on their tongue.

In the early Church there was a very clear sense of the mysterious power of the sacraments, and the radical break a person had to make with his or her previous life to join the Body of Christ. It was the age of mystery religions, of a multitude of exotic oriental cults periodically sweeping the Roman Empire and of secret initiations conducted behind closed doors. The Catholic Church had its secret initiations too – partly because for several centuries to be a Christian was a capital offence. While under instruction, the applicant wanting to join the Church was called a 'catechumen' and, as such, was only allowed to attend the part of the Mass involving the proclamation of Scripture: all catechumens had to leave the church before the divine liturgy reached the Eucharistic prayer, the central mystery of Christianity, into which they had not yet been admitted.

> This food we call Eucharist, no one is allowed to partake of except one who believes that the things we teach are true, and has received the washing for forgiveness of sins and for rebirth, and who lives as Christ handed down to us. For we do not receive these things as common bread or common drink; but as Jesus Christ our Saviour being incarnate by God's word took flesh and blood for our salvation, so also we have been taught that the food consecrated by the word of prayer which comes from him, from which our flesh and blood are nourished by transformation, is the flesh and blood of that incarnate Jesus.
>
> Justin, *Apology* I,66 (2nd century)

The Mass is so important to Catholics because, through the actions of the priest, it enables them to take part in the self-sacrifice of Jesus on the Cross, which he himself anticipated at the Last Supper. The Last Supper is so called because Jesus ate it with his closest disciples just before he was arrested, tried and crucified (knowing what was about to happen). The supper they ate was already a ritual, namely the Jewish Passover meal, which commemorates the time Moses led the Israelites – God's Chosen People – out of slavery in the land of Egypt. Jesus deliberately adapted and transformed this ritual meal into the sacrament that would seal his 'new covenant' with mankind and create a new 'Chosen People' more universal than Israel: the Church. As we read in Matthew (26:26–8), Mark (14:22–4) and Luke (22:17–20), at the supper Jesus identified the bread and wine with his own body and blood, and told his disciples to 'Do this in memory of me'. The Catholic Church has taken him literally on this point, being guided by Jesus's own teaching recorded in the sixth chapter of John's Gospel, where in talking about the Eucharist that he will institute later he insists that this teaching must not be regarded as mere symbolism or 'picture language'. He really means it.

'I am the bread of life. Your fathers ate the manna in the wilderness, and they died. THIS is the bread which comes down from heaven, that a man may eat of it and not die. I am the living bread which came down from heaven; if any one eats of this bread, he will live for ever; and the bread which I shall give for the life of the world is my flesh.' The Jews then disputed among themselves, saying, 'How can this man give us his flesh to eat?' So Jesus said to them, 'Truly, truly, I say to you, unless you eat the flesh of the Son of man and drink his blood, you have no life in you.'

(John 6:48–53).

Catholics believe that when Jesus, and later any priest legitimately acting in his name, with his authority, pronounces those words 'This is my body … This is the cup of my blood' in the context of the Mass, a change comes over the bread and wine, a change that only an all-powerful God could bring about. It does not alter the apparent physical properties of the bread and wine, so we can only know by faith that something has happened. The change involves what the bread and wine *really* are – not what they look like, even under a microscope, but what God transforms them into. They become Jesus. Catholics treat the Blessed Sacrament (the consecrated bread and wine) with great reverence, both within the Mass and afterwards, because they believe God is *really present* in it.

The point of receiving communion – or eating and drinking Christ's body and blood – is to allow Christ to come as close as he can to us, to be as intimately present as the food we eat, as a way of inviting and welcoming his spirit into our hearts. So after receiving communion, most people will feel a natural inclination to sit or kneel quietly and pray, meditating on the presence of Christ within them. Once again, God is using the fact that we are bodily creatures – that he made us this way – in order to communicate with us and transform us. For Catholics also believe that after we die our bodies will somehow be resurrected, like that of Christ himself. It is Christ's resurrected body and blood that we receive in Holy Communion, not his previous earthly body that was subject to death. That resurrected body, invisibly present within us for just a few minutes, is like a token, a promise, of the life to come.

From this fact evolved the practice of Eucharistic adoration or exposition, whereby a previously consecrated host is not eaten but placed in a receptacle called a monstrance and displayed on the altar as the focus of prayer. In medieval times (and in southern European countries today) the monstrance was taken into the streets as the heart of a public procession, perhaps with children scattering petals in front of it as it passed through the town. This practice is reviving in the English-speaking world as people come once more to appreciate the symbolic power of such public devotions.

Protestants have sometimes accused Catholics of worshipping a piece of bread. But wouldn't you worship it if you thought it had ceased to be bread and was actually God? The Eucharist is like the sun in the solar system of the sacraments. By turning towards it, by being receptive towards it, Catholics orientate themselves body and soul towards the very centre and source of life, and their final destination. Eucharistic adoration usually concludes with a service called Benediction, in which the priest lifts up the monstrance and imparts a blessing to the congregation. Christians believe that once God became a child in order to draw near to us: now, Catholics believe, he gives himself over to us in a form even smaller, even more vulnerable than a child.

In the end, all the sacraments can be seen in the context of this outward-moving impetus on the part of God. For Catholics, each embodies the action of the Blessed Trinity in every aspect of human life, falling like gentle rain on the landscape of the human soul. Each sacrament can be traced back to the ministry of the Son in his time on earth, each is imbued with the Holy Spirit, who breathes life into the Church even at the worst moments in her history, and each brings us back to the source of our being, God the Father of all, creator of everything we know, in whose image humanity is so mysteriously said, in Genesis, to be forged.

2

No man is an island: last things and the communion of saints

What the Church calls the 'four last things' are the things that bound our earthly horizon: death, judgement, heaven and hell. These are the things we try to forget. Most of the time we succeed.

Dust to Dust?

Death is the only one of these four that is evident to a non-religious person. But Catholics believe that death was not part of God's original plan for man. It came into the world because of sin and the damage that sin does to the fabric of reality. When in Genesis we are told that God exiles Adam and Eve from the Garden after they eat from the forbidden tree of the 'knowledge of good and evil', in case they reach out 'and take also of the tree of life, and eat, and live for ever' (Genesis 3:22), this was because living for ever while in a state of fallenness would have been an unending tragedy. Instead, they are sent into a realm where death will come to them and bring them back to God for judgement, and Christ is sent into the world to free them from sin by suffering its consequences in himself.

Facing the inevitability of death may make us concerned with what may happen after it. But it also brings us face to face with the question of *who we really are.* For the Catholic, our personal identity involves both body and soul. The soul is the spiritual principle that makes the body into a living whole, instead of just a cluster of cells each doing their own thing. Of course, each cell has its own life cycle and our bodies are changing all the time. On the purely physical level there is no identity from one moment to the next, only a greater or lesser continuity. What makes my body into an expression or manifestation of *me*, even when it changes over time, is the soul. The soul also changes, but not in the same way; rather it changes by the exercise of free will, which is the power of the soul to determine its destiny and destination. For all these reasons Catholics do not believe in reincarnation, which presupposes a much looser connection of body and soul in the identity of the person.

Death is the separation of body from soul. If you have seen a person die, you will probably have felt that something 'departs' and what is left is no longer the person you know. Yet the soul by itself is not the person either, and this is an important aspect of the Catholic belief about death. The soul does survive the body, but it is incomplete without it. At death, the soul leaves the realm of time and decay, and finds itself in a world outside time. It makes little sense to say that the soul finds itself 'temporarily' without a body, because the word 'temporarily' assumes the existence of time. But from our point of view – the point of view of those of us who remain in time – the dead person's soul can be thought of as being in some kind of waiting state until time finally comes to end *for the world as a whole*, when Catholics believe the soul will be reunited with its body and become whole again in a new state of existence.

The Book of Revelation, the last book in the Bible, talks about a new heaven and a new earth, in which God will take what existed before and make it new. We get a glimpse of what this means in the stories about the resurrection of Christ in the Gospels. His body disappeared from the tomb, so it was in a sense the same body that was resurrected that he had before. Yet it was also different. He is not a ghost. He is able to eat and to be touched. But he can suddenly appear and disappear inside a locked room, and his friends do not even recognize him until he performs some familiar action that opens their eyes (such as calling Mary Magdalene by name, or telling Peter and John where to cast their nets).

The risen body is not limited by our space and time, but is in fact the principle of a new space and time. In his Letter to the Corinthians, the Apostle Paul tries to convey something of this when he compares the physical body that dies to a seed. 'What is sown is perishable, what is raised is imperishable. ... As was the man of dust, so are those who are of the dust; and as is the man of heaven, so are those who are of heaven. Just as we have borne the image of the man of dust, we will also bear the image of the man of heaven' (1 Corinthians 15:42–9).

In the Light of Eternity

We do not like to feel 'judged' because the people who judge us do not know us as we know ourselves. It is different with God. The judgement of God coincides exactly with our final judgement of ourselves. Judgement is what happens to us when we are removed from time by death. Being no longer subject to the limitations of the body, spread out in time and space, but instead 'collected together' in a moment of clarity, we are shown what we are and what we have made ourselves to be. We will see this reflected in the eyes of God, when the world of time and space no longer stands in the way of that total and all-seeing vision. This moment is described sometimes as a kind of final choice, for or against God. The choice is made during life and in the moment of judgement we know what that choice is.

The Christian life is, in a sense, one long preparation for that moment. In our earthly life we have a kind of freedom that is bound up with only seeing part of reality, one drop at a time, and we react to this or that event, making one decision after another, weaving the story of our lives across a tapestry whose design is not visible to us until we die. But in the after-life our freedom operates in a different way. We will no longer have the freedom to choose one path or another through the world, or to change the way we are and behave. We will be 'set', fully formed. The new kind of freedom we will possess on the other side of death is a freedom to be what we have become, completely, to enjoy it with all the powers of our new existence in that unimaginable state beyond earthly time and in God.

Catholics believe that there are two permanent states possible after death: hell or heaven. There is also 'purgatory', but this is not a final state, simply a process of purification that most people have to go through on their way to heaven. Looking at ourselves with the eyes of God can be a traumatic process. If when we come to die we are still attached to anything other than God, if we are still fragmented, even if our hearts funda-mentally love him, then those attachments and that fragmentation will be felt as something painful, something that tears us apart. The feeling is described as like being burned with fire. But it is a healthy and good thing, because the pain that comes from seeing the imperfections in our lives is precisely what now detaches us from those imperfections, which is why the fire is described as 'purifying'. It is the love that binds us to God that is experienced as fire.

As for the existence of hell, there isn't much to say, since it is so appalling as to be almost unimaginable. Apart from being taught by the Church, it is a logical conclusion from the doctrine of free will. If you take all I have said about our striving to draw close to God, or at the very least to whatever is good and true and beautiful, and then nix it, you have hell. Hell is the condition of souls who reject God utterly, in practice and in principle. They have no love in them at all. Hell is purely and simply the absence of God, freely chosen and adhered to right to the end. We may hope that it will be empty, even of our enemies, since Christ put himself on the line for this and no Christian would want to waste what happened on the Cross.

Hell will never be truly empty, since its principal denizens are the fallen angels under the leadership of Lucifer, or the Devil. The Catholic Church teaches that once an entirely spiritual being, an angel, has turned against its creator, its decision is final and irrevocable. It has no earthly life in which to repent and change its mind. This is why the Devil and his companions play such a dramatic role in the spiritual struggle of the individual soul. There is a force out there that does not want us to be saved, to be united with God. The machinations of this force have been fascinatingly portrayed by spiritual writers down the ages; C. S. Lewis's *Screwtape Letters* is one of the most readable to modern ears. Tolkien vividly depicts an aspect of this seductive and destructive force in *The Lord of the Rings* as the Dark Lord Sauron.

Contrary to popular belief, Catholics do not believe that everyone outside the Catholic Church is condemned to hell. God works more mysteriously than this and only he knows whether a soul has finally rejected him or not.

The Communion of Saints

Heaven is more interesting than either purgatory or hell. It is, after all, where we hope to end up. Of course, this belies its greeting-card image: clouds, harps and angels in badly designed nighties. I was discussing this with a friend who was close to death and we were laughing over our different conceptions of the place. My vision was of a table laden with food and wine, at which all the people I love were gathered (I wouldn't necessarily have to do the cooking). Her vision was of solitude: being alone with God on a beautiful mountainside. Yet our two partial points of view were not in conflict, ultimately, for we recognized them as just that: partial, incomplete. The essence of our vision was, of course, perfect love. While I often yearn for solitude and peace in spite of my sociable nature, my friend spoke of her appreciation of physical things, the beauty of the sun-drenched springtime around her, the delight she took in eating tasty dishes in spite of her physical condition, the pleasure her husband and children gave her as she contemplated their lives. She also spoke of her growing realization that we share in one another's gifts and it is this sharing that marks out the nature of eternal life. No man is an island. While we can affect one another for the worse, we can also affect one another by our sincere striving to draw close to God.

This is the paradox of heaven, for a Catholic. It is not a material place, yet it contains all that is good in the material life we experience now, only better. And of course one of the best parts of that life is the company of others, those who accompany us in the true quest for God. Those who have achieved the quest are called 'saints'. This term refers to all those who purely and simply are with God, in heaven. Their number is beyond counting, like the stars – like the descendants God promised to Abraham. In the vast night sky, however, there are certain constellations that shine a little more brightly and stars by which we can navigate at sea. These more visible heavenly companions are the 'canonized' saints – the saints officially recognized by the Catholic Church.

For a woman or a man to be canonized by the pope, he or she has to pass through a rigorous process of assessment. All the details of his or her life on earth will be looked at, to see if they display 'heroic virtue'. This does not mean they were perfect from birth. St Paul, St Augustine, St Mary Magdalene – there are many saints who at one time were not what you might think of as saintly. The point is rather that their lives as a whole, redeemed and transformed by Christ, gave overwhelming witness to the glory that comes from him. Different saints reflect that glory in different ways: after all, God is the source of the whole multifarious complexity of creation.

The saints are the ecosystem of the Church, all interconnected in their marvellous diversity. The faithful ask the saints for their 'intercession', that is to say for their prayers before the throne of God, usually in an area where they are recognized to have a special interest. A saint is often called the 'patron' of such and such: St Francis is the patron of ecology, for obvious reasons, St Anthony is often invoked when something lost needs finding. There is even a patron of impossible causes: St Jude.

Being virtuous is one thing, but a candidate for canonization can reach the second stage (being declared 'blessed') only if a miracle can be attributed to his or her intercession, usually a miracle of physical healing, where medical evidence can clearly show a cure without scientific explanation. The holy man or woman must be shown to care for his or her brethren on earth, even after death. 'By their fruits shall you know them,' as Jesus said. To reach the final stage (being declared a saint) a second miracle is needed.

Talk of the 'intercession of the saints' and prayer to the saints tends to make Protestant Christians uncomfortable, so one more word of explanation is needed. It is not that Catholics worship the saints. God is the only object of worship. God is the only one who can answer prayers, or perform miracles that don't obey the normal laws of nature. But Catholics believe that good people who have died are never completely cut off from the rest of us. Being in God, they are still aware of us and our needs. They are in Christ and in him we can touch each other. Why would they not continue to pray for their friends, and for those whose needs they perceive, from heaven? This is the origin of the Catholic practice of praying to the saints, those who love us from heaven, who now see God face to face. We ask them to pray on our behalf to God, or 'intercede' with God for us.

Saints are not VIPs on a red carpet: they are a working body of souls with special responsibilities for those who come after them. They are the most mysterious and glorious way that God shares his very being with his own creatures.

Queen of Heaven

All this talk of the 'last things' and heaven in particular brings us inevitably to the greatest saint of all time, the one who bore the most obviously good fruit, Mary the Mother of Jesus.

The devotion shown by both Catholics and Orthodox towards this human woman is not always well understood. Such things were stripped away by the reformers in the sixteenth century as being contrary to their dependence on Scripture alone. The Litany of Loreto, a prayer that names Mary under titles such as Ark of the Covenant, Vessel of Singular Devotion and Tower of David, the endless hymns and 'Hail Marys' and statues and icons, can all seem excessive to a non-Catholic. At best, you may feel, she is simply another saint: why all the fuss? After all, didn't Our Lord tick off the woman in the crowd who cried out 'Blessed is the womb that bore you, and the breasts that you sucked'? Didn't he correct her, saying 'Blessed rather are those who hear the word of God and keep it' (Luke 11:27–8)?

For Catholics, Mary's importance is due to that essential *incarnational reality* around which the Catholic faith revolves. As Mother Teresa once said, 'No Mary: no Jesus.' In the Gospels, after the infancy narratives, the Mother of Jesus barely makes an appearance until it is time to stand, agonized, under the Cross. In the Gospels it is written that blood and water flowed from Christ's side when the centurion pierced it to ensure that he was dead (John 19:34). This has been woven into the imagery of Christ giving birth to the Church. Mary plays a central role in this moment. Among the last words of her son are those addressed to his Mother and St John the Evangelist, the only male Apostle to have stayed with her at the foot of the Cross. 'Mother, behold your son. Son, behold your mother.' In the Catholic understanding of Scripture, if John standing at the foot of the Cross represents all faithful Christians, the woman who is given to him as mother in that moment can be called nothing less than 'mother of the Church', mother of all who follow her Son. Mary represents discipleship: this is the real meaning of that seeming rebuke directed by Jesus against those who thought Mary's physical relationship to Jesus could be more important than a spiritual one.

To 'hear my word and keep it' is the very definition of what it means to follow Christ. The notion of the 'word' is central to the Christian mystery. It means both the literal word, the command of God ('If anyone loves me he will keep my word') and the Word Incarnate, Jesus himself. St John begins his Gospel, which focuses so closely on that double meaning: 'In the beginning was the Word, and the Word was with God.' By virtue of her 'keeping' this word, that is to say paying attention to her Son's teaching and putting it into practice, Mary is the very first Christian. Mary is said to have conceived Jesus first not in her womb, but in her heart and soul, by being receptive to the angel's promise and by being willing to do all that God asked of her. Her physical motherhood was contingent on that spiritual relationship, even as the spiritual relationship needed her physical motherhood to achieve its true meaning. The story of the Annunciation in the Gospel of Luke paints a minimalist, yet powerful, picture of her character.

In the sixth month the angel Gabriel was sent from God to a city of Galilee named Nazareth, to a virgin betrothed to a man whose name was Joseph, of the house of David and the virgin's name was Mary. And he came to her and said, 'Hail, full of grace, the Lord is with you!' But she was greatly troubled at the saying, and considered in her mind what sort of greeting this might be. And the angel said to her, 'Do not be afraid, Mary, for you have found favour with God. And behold, you will bear a son, and you shall call his name Jesus. He will be great, and will be called the Son of the Most High: and the Lord God will give to him the throne of his father David, and he will reign over the house of Jacob for ever; and of his kingdom there will be no end.'

Luke 1:26–33

When told she was to conceive, Mary's first response was to ask a perfectly logical question: 'How can this be, since I have no husband?' Once assured by the angel of the purely super-natural nature of the conception to take place, she stands down her question and simply accepts the invitation. It is hard, with-out putting oneself in her shoes – the difficulties involved in that time and place, the scandal that would be caused to her family, the perturbing mystery she will be harbouring so inti-mately within her own body and her own home – fully to appreciate the enormity of this straightforward consent, this act of faith, her *fiat* (the Latin word for 'let it be'): 'Behold, I am the handmaid of the Lord: let it be to me according to your word.' This acceptance is exactly the act of faith that makes her at once the first Christian believer and the physical locus of the Incarnation. The two things are inextricably linked in her from the very start.

The Church Fathers called Mary Theotokos, 'God-bearer' or Mother of God, in order to emphasize that, like every mother, she was the mother not just of the body of her child but of the whole person, even though in her case that person was divine (Council of Ephesus, 431). In this way the Fathers tried to emphasize the unity of human and divine nature in

Jesus Christ against those who wanted to separate them. Marian doctrine developed from there. In other words the Catholic doctrines about Mary were developed partly as a way of defending fundamental Christian beliefs about Jesus.

Since the Reformation in the sixteenth century, Catholic devotion to Mary has become a bone of contention. Not all Christians, for example, accept the idea of Mary's immaculate conception (meaning that she was conceived without original sin), her perpetual virginity (meaning that she remained a virgin even after bearing Jesus), or her bodily assumption into heaven at the end of her earthly life. Nevertheless each of these doctrines is for Catholics only the logical outcome of a millennia-long reflection on the meaning of her life.

The doctrine of the Immaculate Conception was one of the most debated teachings in the history of the Church and it received a formal definition only in 1854, by Pope Pius IX.

'We declare, pronounce and define that the doctrine which holds that the Blessed Virgin Mary, at the first instant of her conception, by a singular privilege and grace of the Omnipotent God, in virtue of the merits of Jesus Christ, the Saviour of mankind, was preserved immaculate from all stain of original sin, has been revealed by God, and therefore should firmly and constantly be believed by all the faithful.'

Pius IX, *Ineffabilis Deus*, 8 December 1854

Interestingly, the spiritual impetus for this came not from intellectuals and expert theologians, but from a completely different source. In 1830 a young nun called Catherine Labouré, a novice with the Daughters of Charity in Paris, brought up in the countryside with very little education, saw a series of apparitions of the Blessed Virgin. She was instructed to have a medal made, with the words engraved on it: 'O Mary, conceived without sin, pray for us who have recourse to thee.' This came to be known as the Miraculous Medal and is worn by a huge number of the faithful.

In 1858 an even less educated young peasant in the Pyrenees, called Bernadette Soubirous, also saw visions of the Blessed Virgin. When asked who she was, Mary replied: 'I am the Immaculate Conception.' Bernadette had never heard the words before and her parish priest, knowing the dogma had just been declared, was astounded. The lasting legacy of this series of apparitions was the miraculous spring of water discovered at the place Mary indicated to the young Bernadette. This source is now a major pilgrimage site for Catholics: Lourdes, where many people have been healed in body or soul.

The doctrine of the Assumption took even longer to define, being proclaimed by the pope only as late as 1950, although the idea itself had been around for a very long time. At St Catherine's monastery on Mount Sinai, there is a seventh-century manuscript of a homily by Theoteknos, Bishop of Livias in Palestine, which contains a very clear indication of what many early Christians already believed about Mary. 'The assumption of the body of the holy one, and her ascension to heaven, took place on the fifteenth day of August, which is the sixth day of the month of Mesore. And there was joy in heaven and on earth, as the angels struck up the hymn, while human beings glorified the mother of the King of Heaven, who had herself glorified the human race: the Mother of God.' There is an 'eschatological' aspect to this doctrine, which means that it reveals something about the ultimate destiny of humanity, a destiny in which the body plays a vital role in the great cosmological scheme.

The importance of Mary in the daily life of Catholics is expressed best in the 'Hail Mary', which is one of the most common prayers in the Catholic tradition. It expresses in a few lines Catholic devotion to Mary. It goes like this:

> Hail Mary, full of grace, the Lord is with thee.
> Blessed art thou among women, and blessed is the fruit of thy womb, Jesus.
> Holy Mary, Mother of God, pray for us sinners, now and at the hour of our death.

The name of Jesus is placed right at the heart of the prayer, which is itself based mostly on quotations from the Gospels. The prayer is a humble request to the Virgin to pray for us to God. The 'Hail Mary' is often prayed in a sequence of repetitions called the Rosary, measured out on a string of beads, accompanied by other prayers, especially the 'Our Father', the 'Glory Be' and meditations on the life of Christ. Many people find this a powerful form of meditation – a way of meditating on Jesus through the eyes of Mary that originated in the medieval era, possibly with St Dominic.

When Catholics think of the Last Things, when they face the reality of their own death and what will happen to them afterwards, their minds turn to the Blessed Virgin Mary, through whom their Saviour was born, trusting that she will be the mother that he promised she would be when he hung on the Cross, and help them be faithful to him.

Standing by the cross of Jesus were His mother, and His mother's sister, Mary the wife of Clopas, and Mary Magdalene. When Jesus saw His mother, and the disciple whom He loved standing near, He said to His mother, 'Woman, behold your son!' Then He said to the disciple, 'Behold, your mother!' And from that hour the disciple took her to his own home.

John 19:25–7

3

The paradox of the papacy

By writing about the sacraments, the saints and the Virgin Mary before speaking about the Catholic Church as a powerful worldwide institution, I have deliberately put what I consider to be the most important aspects of the faith first. Yet when non-Catholics look at the Church, they more often see it 'sociologically'. They see it as a human organization, a social body. They may hate it or admire it, envy it for its influence and riches, or despise it for corrupting the minds of millions. They may love it for preserving Western civilization, or for defending the poor countries of the Third World. But what they are reacting to is definitely an 'it', a thing, an organization with members and managers. In a moment I will explain why the Church is much more than an 'it' to Catholics – why they think of it as a 'she', a mother like the Virgin Mary, even though it is governed by celibate males, but for now I will take the institutional view.

The Catholic Church is the largest (and longest surviving) of all religious institutions on the face of the planet. She comprises today about 1,200 million people, a sixth of the world's population (and half of all Christians). All of them technically owe allegiance to the pope or 'Holy Father', the Bishop of Rome who is elected to his position for life by a 'college' of cardinals (a select group of priests and bishops appointed by previous popes). The pope is also the head of a small city-state called the Vatican, which is located in Rome but not governed by Italy and whose largest building is the giant basilica of St Peter (believed to be built over the tomb of the Apostle Peter, who was the first pope).

Around the pope are gathered the men and women (mostly men) he chooses to run the various departments of the Church, known as the 'curia'. But the day-to-day running of the Church on the ground around the world is entrusted to the various local archbishops and, slightly below them in the hierarchy, the bishops. The territory ruled by a bishop is called a diocese and several dioceses make up each archdiocese. In England and Wales, for example, there are twenty-two dioceses and four archdioceses. Bishops are regarded as the successors of the Apostles (the first priests consecrated by Christ and entrusted with the care of his disciples). Down on 'ground level', each diocese is divided into parishes, and each parish has a priest in charge – around three thousand in England and Wales serving four million Catholic parishioners. (Things are slightly more complicated than this if you take into account the existence of the various Eastern churches that have slightly different traditions and rites, but also owe allegiance to the pope; these are known as the Uniate Churches.)

The Church virtually invented the term 'subsidiarity', describing the principle of devolved government, which is how it is able to operate on such a huge scale right across the world: decisions are generally made at the parish level, coordinated where necessary from above – and, of course, appeal can always be made higher up if there is a dispute. The archbishops, and above them the pope, do not drive the great ship of the Church like an engine, because it runs itself, but they do help to turn the rudder.

So much for the institution of the Church. It is important, but it is not the whole story and, for me, by no means the most interesting part. In this chapter I will be glancing at one aspect of the history of the Church, that is to say the Petrine or papal ministry, which means taking Peter, the first pope, and his successors as a thread that holds the whole story together. But I want you to remember what I said about the Virgin Mary and the sacraments. The Church exists in order to protect and administer the sacraments, which are the source of Catholic spirituality, the main way that we connect with the earthly life of Jesus Christ. And the Virgin Mary is at the heart of the Church, superior both in power and in holiness to the priestly hierarchies and the pope himself.

How is that possible? To understand it, and to see the history of the Church as a Catholic does, we have to look first at the role of the Holy Spirit, for the Spirit is the link between God, Mary and the Church. From the Old Testament to the New, the role of this mysterious Spirit of God is woven through the narrative. The Spirit hovers above the primal waters at the beginning of time, is breathed into Adam, speaks through the prophets, until at last he can hover above another sea (Latin: *maris*), the 'sea' of the virgin's womb. Through the power of the Holy Spirit the Virgin Mary conceives the Christ child, the long-awaited Messiah. For that reason Mary is sometimes called the 'spouse' of the Holy Spirit (even though, in earthly terms, she was married to Joseph). It is a way of indicating how intimately she and the Holy Spirit were united in the act of conceiving Christ.

At Jesus's baptism and his transfiguration, the Holy Spirit

appears to him and after his resurrection from death he tells his disciples: 'You shall receive power when the Holy Spirit has come upon you: and you shall be my witnesses in Jerusalem and in all Judaea and Samaria and to the end of the earth' (Acts 1:8). This occurred forty days after the resurrection. Ten days later, on the feast of Pentecost (meaning fifty days), the Book of Acts describes how the Holy Spirit descended like 'a rushing wind and tongues of fire' upon the disciples as they waited and prayed with Mary the Mother of Jesus in a hidden room in Jerusalem. The coming of the Holy Spirit sends the Apostles out into the world to preach: the Church is born. And Mary is there: reminding us that she is Mother to the Church by being the Mother of Jesus who is the head of the Church – by the power of the Holy Spirit working in her.

Mary and the Holy Spirit: two of the three keys to Church history. That history begins with Mary, the first Christian, disciple of her own son. But Mary would not be holy, would not be the Mother of Christ, without the Holy Spirit, who is the presence and action of God within her soul and body – the same Spirit who led Israel's prophets to the threshold of the New Covenant and who makes the Church through history a place to encounter God in the sacraments.

The Peter Paradigm

So what can we say of Peter, the third key to Church history, known as the 'Keeper of the Keys'?

Each of us has a living spirit within us, but we also have bones and organs and tissues: the Church likewise. And just as the structure of the human body is hierarchical, with the head and the heart at the centre on which the rest of the body depends, so the Church is a hierarchy, with Peter playing a central role among the Apostles. Acts 2:41 tells how the Holy Spirit inspires Peter, a simple fisherman, to assume the leadership role – the office of 'Rock' – that Christ earlier appointed for him (see box).

> Simon Peter replied, 'You are the Christ, the Son of the living God.' And Jesus answered him, 'Blessed are you, Simon Bar-Jona! For flesh and blood has not revealed this to you, but my Father who is in heaven. And I tell you, you are Peter, and on this rock [the name 'Peter' means 'rock'] I will build my church, and the powers of death shall not prevail against it. I will give you the keys of the kingdom of heaven, and whatever you bind on earth shall be bound in heaven, and whatever you loose on earth shall be loosed in heaven.'
>
> Matthew 16:16–19

History would be nothing without people. The history of the Church is bound up with, and reflected in, the life stories of her saints. By looking at the saints, Catholics believe, we can better understand the Church. Thus it makes sense that the story of Peter as recorded in Scripture would in some sense foreshadow, and help us to understand, exactly how that office of leader, later called 'pope', bestowed upon him by Christ, would evolve throughout history.

In the early days of following Jesus, Peter is filled with enthusiasm, but does not always understand what Jesus is trying to get across. He tries to copy Jesus walking on water, begins to sink and has to be rescued: 'O man of little faith! Why did you doubt?' (Matthew 14:25–31). Peter comes over as a devoted but impulsive man. In the Gospel of Matthew, immediately after the account of Peter's profession of faith that I quoted above, we hear how Peter still got hold of the wrong end of the stick, insisting that Jesus should not have to go to his death in Jerusalem. For this he incurred an amazingly severe rebuke: 'Get behind me Satan! You are a hindrance to me; for you are not on the side of God, but of men.'

This rebuke, however, makes sense in the context of the whole discourse, where Jesus underlines that redemption will take place through suffering. 'If any man would come after me, let him deny himself and take up his cross and follow me. For whoever would save his life will lose it, and whoever loses his life for my sake will find it. For what will it profit a man, if he gains the whole world and forfeits his life? Or what shall a man give in return for his life?' (Matthew 16:24–6). The force that tempts Peter, or even Jesus himself (who, while he never gave in to it, was nonetheless tempted, as in the forty days in the desert at the beginning of his public ministry), is the original temptation of Genesis, all over again: 'You shall be as gods …' That is to say, the easy way out, the way of power and self-gratification, turning one's back on God in order to set oneself up as the arbiter and main player in the drama of salvation.

What we are seeing here is a portrait not just of Peter, but of the whole papacy and the temptations that later popes would often succumb to, at times almost destroying the institution.

Immediately after the challenge laid down by Jesus in the Gospel of Matthew we have the account of his 'transfiguration', in which Peter, James and John receive a vision of the Lord in the glory to which he had referred just before.

And after six days Jesus took with him Peter and James and John his brother, and led them up a high mountain apart. And he was transfigured before them, and his face shone like the sun, and his garments became white as light. And behold, there appeared to them Moses and Elijah, talking with him. And Peter said to Jesus, 'Lord, it is well that we are here; if you wish, I will make three booths here, one for you and one for Moses and one for Elijah.' He was still speaking, when lo, a bright cloud overshadowed them, and a voice from the cloud said, 'This is my beloved Son, with whom I am well pleased; listen to him.' When the disciples heard this, they fell on their faces, and were filled with awe. But Jesus came and touched them, saying, 'Rise, and have no fear.' And when they lifted up their eyes, they saw no one but Jesus only.

Matthew 17:1–8

Here Peter is accorded the privilege of seeing and understanding the truth precisely while remaining a fallible, even rather bumbling, human being. The suggestion of building booths for the three figures of the vision is all too human: how often have we sought to capture, freeze or hold on to a privileged moment in our lives, as though we could make it our possession? It is rather like whipping out your camera and taking a picture of the person who has just declared undying love for you. And this time the corrective comes from the Father himself – a reiteration of what Peter knows, that this is indeed the Son of God, but also a reminder: 'Listen to him.' In other words when Jesus says, *Let go, don't cling to your preconceived ideas, don't try to possess the moment, just live it, let it transform you*, those who love him are solemnly enjoined to pay attention.

It is not surprising that Peter, and those who after him headed up the Church in succeeding years, have frequently lost sight of this fundamental principle. It is hard for someone constantly to remember that his power is a supernatural, rather than a worldly, affair. But the most successful popes have been the ones who have maintained the supernatural vision of what they are doing, who have attempted to listen to what God is telling them, rather than trying to force the revelation of this reality into an ideological straitjacket.

Not of this World: the Ultimate Priorities of Peter

There are other passages which, if read with an eye to this principle, are highly instructive with regard to Peter's role. For instance, there is the Gethsemane episode in the eighteenth chapter of the Gospel of John. Judas Iscariot, who has betrayed Jesus to the authorities, arrives with soldiers to arrest Jesus. Peter wishes to defend his master: with a sword, no less. He cuts off the ear of the servant of the high priest, Malchus.

Jesus rebukes Peter for this act of violence, even in defence of his master. 'Shall I not drink of the cup?' he asks – having only a short while earlier pleaded with his Father to remove that very cup of suffering he is about to receive. Jesus then heals the ear of the servant. Later, when Jesus is handed over to Pilate, the Roman governor asks if he is claiming to be a king. Jesus answers, 'My kingship is not of this world. If my kingship were of this world, my servants would fight, that I might not be handed over to the Jews; but my kingship is not from this world.' This is curious, because one of his followers, namely

Peter, has indeed tried to fight to keep him from being handed over.

If we look forward in history, we see that some of Peter's successors were perfectly prepared to take up the sword in the name of Christ. We have all heard of the Wars of Religion. Yet Jesus rebuked Peter for this. And the violence done by the Church has certainly prevented many people from being able to 'hear' the word of God. Yet in the Gospel story Jesus heals the victim of Peter's aggression, restoring his ear. The importance of this symbolism is reinforced by the reported exchange between Pilate and Jesus that follows in the same Gospel. When Pilate asks him if he is a king, Jesus answers, 'You say I am a king. For this I was born and for this I came into the world, to testify to the truth. Everyone who belongs to the truth *listens to my voice.*'

Straightforward violence is not the only mistake Peter makes. Between the scuffle with the high priest's servant and the conversation with Pilate, there is the excruciating passage in which Peter, hanging around for news while the high priest and his cohorts question Jesus, is rumbled by some onlookers: 'Aren't you with the Nazarene?' Peter denies it. They persist – he denies it again. The very act of violence he committed earlier is brought up as evidence of his true identity. But Peter denies his link with Jesus – for the final time. Hearing the cock crow he realizes he has done just what Jesus predicted he would do: denied his master three times.

This helps us to understand how Catholics see the fact that God permits bad popes in the history of the Church, whose actions, if not their words, have seemed to deny Christ. Corrupt popes such as Alexander VI (1492–1503), whose wars, nepotism and sexual orgies brought the Church to its lowest ever point, betrayed Christ on a much more dramatic and gigantic scale than Peter ever did, yet the Catholic can see this as the projection of Peter's story on to the 'big screen' of history. There have been many popes who have been more interested in earthly power than in serving God, who have been prepared to draw the sword, or have others draw it on their behalf, just as though Christ's kingdom were entirely of this world.

But it would be one-sided to recall this if we did not also recall another passage in John's Gospel when the risen Christ speaks to Peter by the side of that lake where he had originally invited him to give up everything to follow him. 'Do you love me?' he asks and Peter assures him he does. A second time he asks the question and Peter repeats his assurance. Then a third time – and Peter becomes desperate. 'Lord, you know everything; you know that I love you.' And at each affirmation, each cancelling out one of the earlier three denials, Jesus anchors Peter's commitment with a very specific command: 'Feed my lambs … tend my sheep … feed my sheep' (John 21:15–17) – the lambs and sheep representing each member of the Church, fed by Peter in the seasons of life between birth and death. Peter is specifically asked to take on the mantle of the original Good Shepherd.

This too, then, is in the DNA of the papacy. No matter what failures its incumbents have been guilty of, Christ always brings Peter back to his senses – and in doing so reminds him of the central point. He must prove his love for the Lord by truly caring for his flock. The majority of popes have been like this, whatever their personal shortcomings. Over time, the plus and minus points of different pontiffs balance each other out. Certainly in modern times, when the Church has lost much of her worldly power, we have witnessed a succession of remarkably holy and able pontiffs. It is worth noting that at the end of the second millennium of Christianity, Pope John Paul II insisted on issuing an apology on behalf of his forebears for sins committed in previous centuries in the name of the Church.

Infallibility

So the Gospels help us to understand the kind of leadership role adopted by Peter, the first pope, and his successors, including the ways in which that leadership can go wrong. But does the Gospel also help us to understand the claim of the pope to be 'infallible'? In fact, doesn't what I have just said prove that the pope is just as fallible as anyone else?

In order to answer that you have to know what the Church means by 'infallibility'. It sounds very grand, but it does not mean that the pope cannot commit serious sins, any more than it means he cannot make mistakes in arithmetic, or politics, or logic.

What Catholics believe about the infallibility of the Pope was 'defined' or clarified in 1870 by the First Vatican Council. The Council said that the pope, when he teaches *ex cathedra* (meaning from the throne of Peter, i.e. formally to the whole Church, not just in his bedroom or round the breakfast table), 'enjoys, by reason of the Divine assistance promised to him in blessed Peter, that infallibility with which the Divine Redeemer wished His Church to be endowed in defining doctrine regarding faith and morals' (Session IV, cap. 4).

The definition doesn't actually give the pope much power at all. It says that all he can do infallibly is confirm and clarify a part of Revelation that has always been there. Anything else he does or says, including making war on France or burning heretics, does not come under the definition. And it stands to reason that any proclamation of a teaching that differs from the doctrines previously infallibly taught by the Church (which covers the whole received faith of the Church) cannot be infallible even if the pope thinks it is.

But why is the pope said to exercise this power (if it is a

power) on his own? Simply because it is his job to represent the whole College of Bishops, which in turn represents the whole People of God, and it is this People that is being kept faithful to the truth by the Holy Spirit. The buck has to stop somewhere and the only way the Church as a whole can be kept from falling into error, when an argument arises over some doctrine, is if there is a way of resolving it: that is why the pope has the deciding vote. And there have been occasions, as we shall see in the next chapter, when such disputes have arisen and a deciding vote has had to be cast. Catholics believe that the Holy Spirit, on those occasions, protects the Church from falling into error – because otherwise how would Christ's promise that the 'powers of death' (other translations say 'the gates of hell') shall not prevail against the Church (Matthew 16:18) be fulfilled.

The presence of the Spirit in the Church functions a bit like the soul in your body, keeping you alive, joining all your different cells together into a single organism. In it many people become one person, whom Catholics call the Bride of Christ, by virtue of their common Spirit. (That person becomes most clearly visible in the Virgin Mary.) But, again just like your own body, parts are dying all the time and dropping away, as the soul preserves the balance of the whole.

In formally defining the Assumption of Mary in the middle of the twentieth century, Pius XII wrote, 'The Holy Ghost was not promised to the successors of Peter in such a way that, by His Revelation, they might manifest new doctrine, but so that, by His assistance, they might guard as sacred and might faithfully propose the revelation delivered through the apostles, or the deposit of faith.' It is this careful, logical unfolding of the faith entrusted to the Apostles, in a living tradition nourished by the real presence of Christ, that best represents 'what Catholics believe'.

4

Two thousand years of history

During the first three centuries of the Church's life, Christians
were regarded as subversive anarchists because of their refusal to
worship Roman gods, including the emperor himself. Several
emperors, beginning with Nero in the first century, to Decius,
Diocletian and Galerius at the beginning of the fourth, perse-
cuted them savagely. Nonetheless, the Church continued to
grow underground, until the conversion of the Emperor
Constantine led to Christianity becoming the official religion of
the Empire. Constantine reigned from 306 to 337 and is said to
have converted after having seen a vision of the *chi-rho*, a cross-
like symbol formed by superimposing the first two letters of the
word 'Christ' in Greek, leading him to victory in the battle of
the Milvian Bridge in 312 (a year later the emperor officially
commanded the toleration of Christians in the Edict of Milan).
This is usually considered to be the turning point towards a
Christian empire.

The Early Councils

In the early Christian centuries it was necessary to work out exactly what faith in Jesus implied and how the Scriptures were to be collated and interpreted. This was done and continues to be done through the work of Ecumenical Councils, official gatherings of members of the Church's official teaching body (the bishops from around the world), in which, under the guidance of the Holy Spirit, doctrinal questions are clarified and resolved insofar as is possible. The first such council is described in the New Testament Book of Acts (chapter 15) and took place in Jerusalem. The Emperor Constantine summoned the next council, that of Nicaea, in 325 and it was followed by six others in the next five centuries that are accepted by nearly all Christians as authoritative (some later councils were accepted by Roman Catholics but not the Orthodox Church, for example). During these councils certain interpretations of the faith were rejected as 'heretical' (from a word meaning 'choice' – the implication being that a heretic is someone who chooses what to believe instead of accepting the faith handed down by the Church). The authority for deciding what was true and what was not lay in the Holy Spirit, who Catholics believe had been entrusted to the whole Church and to the bishops as the Church's leaders, with the pope as the final arbiter.

Heresies are interesting, because they highlight the struggle of human minds to grasp and converse about a faith in its entirety. It is human nature to emphasize one aspect of a broader picture, on account of one's own particular concerns or prejudices and the influence of the philosophies of one's own age. This tendency gave rise to a number of lopsided interpretations of the faith, not just in the early centuries of the Church, but later in history as well. However, in the early centuries the struggle to define and exclude these heresies was often the impelling force behind the formulation of the actual faith and the development of theology.

The First Council of Nicaea, for instance, produced the Nicene Creed as an attempt to refute the Arian heresy, which taught that the Son of God was not himself fully divine. At one time this extremely popular heresy persuaded nearly all the bishops and also the emperor. When bishops themselves are divided, it is the pope who has to hold firm or resolve the issue, until the theologians are able to demonstrate the greater coherence and subtlety of orthodox doctrine. In the case of Arianism, Pope Libellus stood with St Athanasius against the heretic Arius and, although the dispute dragged on for more than a century, subsequent councils confirmed the Nicene position (the full divinity of Christ), culminating in the Council of Chalcedon in 451, during the pontificate of Leo I.

THE NICENE CREED

(The common modern translation by the English Language Liturgical Commission)

We believe in one God, the Father, the Almighty,
maker of heaven and earth, of all that is, seen and unseen.
We believe in one Lord, Jesus Christ, the only Son of God,
eternally begotten of the Father, God from God, Light from Light,
true God from true God, begotten, not made, of one Being with the Father.
Through him all things were made.

For us men and for our salvation he came down from heaven:
by the power of the Holy Spirit he became incarnate from
the Virgin Mary,
and was made man.
For our sake he was crucified under Pontius Pilate: he
suffered death and was buried.
On the third day he rose again in accordance with the
Scriptures:
he ascended into heaven and is seated at the right hand of
the Father.
He will come again in glory to judge the living and the dead,
and his kingdom will have no end.
We believe in the Holy Spirit, the Lord, the giver of life,
who proceeds from the Father and the Son.
With the Father and the Son he is worshipped and
glorified.
He has spoken through the Prophets.
We believe in one holy catholic and apostolic Church.
We acknowledge one baptism for the forgiveness of sins.
We look for the resurrection of the dead, and the life of the
world to come.
Amen.

The Formation of Christendom

'Christendom' simply means a political society in which
Christianity is the established religion. The Christian empire
founded by Constantine I divided after his death into East and
West, with Constantine's city Constantinople (formerly Byzantium, now Istanbul) as the centre of the Eastern empire. The

Western empire based in Rome went into decline and was overrun by barbarian tribes out of Asia, Rome itself being sacked by Visigoths and Vandals in the fifth century. But the barbarians themselves were gradually won over to Christianity and Western Europe witnessed the development of a new Christian civilization, united for a brief while under Charlemagne, who took the title emperor and was crowned by the pope as such on Christmas day in the year 800.

It is easy to say, from our vantage point, that the Church should never have been allied with political power in the first place, but it would have been difficult for the pope to do anything else in the circumstances that prevailed after the decline of the Roman Empire. Neither Constantine nor Charlemagne, to name the two most powerful instigators of political conditions favourable to spreading the faith, was exactly saintly, but even so they protected the Church sufficiently for her to operate as a civilizing influence in the midst of social and political chaos.

First Schism

By the second millennium certain differences had developed between the Western (Latin) Church based in Rome and the Eastern (Greek) Church based in Constantinople/Byzantium. In the West the Church tended to define itself as 'Catholic' (meaning universal rather than localized or 'national'), whereas in the East Christians tended to define themselves as 'Orthodox' (meaning 'right-thinking'). One of the arguments between them concerned the insertion by the Latin Church of an extra word into the Creed, to which the Orthodox objected. The word in question was *filioque*, meaning 'and the Son'. The earlier versions of the Creed had asserted that the Holy Spirit proceeded from the

Father. The extra word meant that the Spirit proceeded from the Father *and the Son*. Even today, some extreme groups among the Orthodox claim that this gives rise to a different conception of God, although most theologians agree it was all a storm in a teacup, reflecting two ways of describing the very same Trinity.

In 1054 an argument about titles and jurisdiction led the pope and the Orthodox patriarch to sever relations, and although the crusades began with the Eastern patriarch's appeal to the West for help against the Turks, the break (known as a 'schism') was consolidated in 1204 when a Venetian-led crusading army diverted from the Holy Land to ransack Constantinople in a brutal display of Christian barbarism against fellow Christians. The Eastern empire survived, though in severe decline, until it was finally conquered by the Ottoman Turks in 1453. The Orthodox Church, led by its own local patriarchs and owing no allegiance to Rome, survived in Greece, the Middle East and also in Russia and elsewhere up to the present. Since the Second Vatican Council in the 1960s there have been many attempts to heal the breach with Catholicism. Many Catholic theologians think that the faith of the Orthodox Church and the Catholic Church is essentially the same.

The Rise of Medieval Monasticism

During the time of the barbarian invasions of Eastern Europe, civilization and literacy were kept going largely by isolated communities of monks and nuns. These were Christians who had dedicated their lives to celibacy and prayer – following in the footsteps of the Eastern desert fathers who had left the cities in the first few centuries after Christ. The Celtic Church of Ireland and Scotland was created by such charismatic figures, while in

Italy St Benedict (d. 543) developed a Rule that was to regulate monastic life throughout Western Europe and would shape the intellectual contours of the new Christian societies that were emerging out of the rubble of the Western empire. Charlemagne called on these monks to build a system of education that eventually gave rise to the first universities.

Monastic foundations were not only important centres of learning, but also provided medical and other material assistance to the surrounding population. While their increasingly large land holdings eventually aroused jealousy among those who thought the orders too powerful, they provided models of agricultural husbandry unrivalled anywhere else in the Christian world at the time. To some extent the monastic communities acted as one of the great equalizing forces in medieval society. This applies also to women, who could wield real authority and control over their destiny in the context of the monastic life. The religious life offered a viable alternative to marriage, and the abbess or 'mother' of a convent wielded an authority equivalent to that of an abbot or bishop.

Throughout the Middle Ages religious women were sought out for their wisdom and known for their mystical visions. Sometimes, like Hildegard of Bingen or Catherine of Siena, they would not hesitate to reprimand even popes for their misdeeds. These women were partly responsible for keeping alive the prophetic tradition in the Church.

The Crusades

The Church tried unsuccessfully to tame the militaristic impulses of the barbarian tribes that had been assimilated into Christendom, imposing more and more rules of combat and restrictions on the number of days per year that fighting was allowed to take place. The 'Peace' or 'Truce of God' prevented fighting on holy days and weekends, protected innocent bystanders and allowed rules of asylum. In 1095 the pope tried to channel the remaining military energies of Europe into a crusade to recapture the holy places associated with the life of Christ from the Turks in Palestine, while in Spain the Moors occupying the peninsula were fought back in a 'reconquest' that culminated in 1492 with the taking of Granada in the south.

The First Crusade to the Holy Land was successful, but only for a time, before the Muslims regained Jerusalem. Subsequent attempts to win back the lost territory proved disastrous. A great deal of the failure of the crusades can, with the benefit of hindsight, be attributed to the lack of moral consistency among many crusaders. While some of those who fought to ensure the Christian presence in the Holy Land were motivated by genuine faith and chivalric idealism, others were simply in it for personal profit. While there were times when Christian knights and Muslim potentates lived in harmony, even sharing the best of the two civilizations, at other times shocking breaches of St Augustine's 'Just War' criteria occurred.

THE CATHOLIC THEORY OF JUST WAR

The following criteria must be satisfied in order to override the strong presumption against the use of force:
Just Cause: force may be used only to correct a serious public evil, e.g. massive violation of the basic rights of whole populations.
Comparative Justice: the injustice suffered by one party

must significantly outweigh that suffered by the other (there may be rights and wrongs on all sides).

Legitimate Authority: only duly constituted public authorities may use deadly force.

Right Intention: force may be used only in a truly just cause.

Probability of Success: arms may not be used in a futile cause or where the means of achieving success is likely to cause even worse problems.

Proportionality: the overall destruction expected from the use of force must be outweighed by the good to be achieved.

Last Resort: force may be used only after all peaceful alternatives have been seriously tried and exhausted.

The just-war tradition seeks also to curb the violence of war by imposing the following moral standards:

Noncombatant Immunity: civilians may not be the object of direct attack, and indirect harm to civilians must be minimized.

Proportionality: no more force than is militarily necessary must be used, and collateral damage to civilian life and property minimized.

Right Intention: the aim of political and military leaders must always be peace with justice, so acts of vengeance and indiscriminate violence are forbidden.

The debacle of the Fourth Crusade, mentioned earlier, brought this tragic strand of Church history to its lowest point. Launched in 1201, the endeavour became mired in political and economic considerations. After discovering what the crusaders did at Constantinople (which had happened against his orders, though he did not do enough to prevent it), Pope Innocent III spoke of divine retribution against the wayward crusaders. Unsurprisingly, none of the subsequent crusading ventures achieved the ultimate aim of regaining control of the holy places in the Middle East.

A Medieval Revolution: the Friars

By 1200 two new 'mendicant' (wandering) religious orders had sprung up to supplement the more stationary Benedictines who had taken vows of stability and stayed in one place to tend a specific monastery and the surrounding land. St Francis and St Dominic preached the Gospel in poverty, on the move, and this new style of spirituality appealed to vast numbers of ordinary people. By joining these orders, whole villages and towns could become exempt from the duty of military service to the local lord and this helped to undermine the feudal system at a time when the merchant class was on the rise. An alternative to the crusades, the non-violent 'Gospel chivalry' of St Francis and the brilliant preaching of the Dominicans helped to humanize and civilize a violent society at the end of the twelfth century. Great artists, scientists, philosophers and theologians belonged to or were connected with these orders, such as Giotto, Fra Angelico, Albert the Great, Bonaventure, Thomas Aquinas.

St Francis founded a fellowship of men (his follower St Clare did the equivalent for women) who vowed to live their lives in poverty and service of all creatures, after a pattern as close as possible to that of Christ. The importance of this renewal to the entire Church was perceived by the pope, who had a dream in which he saw Francis single-handedly propping up the Lateran

Cathedral in Rome, which is where the pope mainly resided before the construction of the Vatican Palace next to St Peter's in the late fourteenth century. Francis constantly put his body on the line for the sake of Christ, even to the point of travelling to the Holy Land, crossing behind enemy lines and entering unarmed into dialogue with the Muslim powers at Acre. Towards the end of his life, while meditating on Christ's passion on the mountain of La Verna north of Assisi, Francis received the stigmata, marks mirroring the wounds of Christ in his hands, feet and side.

St Dominic founded his order in response to the spread of the Cathars in southern France and northern Italy. The Cathars revived a heresy called 'dualism', the belief that the material and spiritual world are opposed, and that the material world could not be the work of an all-powerful, perfectly good Creator God, but must be the work of some lesser deity. St Dominic saw that the pomp and prestige of ecclesiastical representatives made no impact on the population, who were much more impressed by the ascetical lives of the Cathar 'perfecti'. He launched an alternative, though arduous, way of winning back hearts and minds. He and his followers tramped the roads of the Languedoc with no money and no possessions, relying on divine providence and human generosity for their bed and board, preaching the Gospel and entering into dialogue with all they encountered.

Renaissance and Reformation

The flowering of European civilization from 1100 to 1300 was blighted by plague, famine and schism in the fourteenth century, but the Gothic cathedrals built in this time remind us of the great heights attained. The next flowering of Christian culture came in the fifteenth and sixteenth centuries, as the rediscovery of pagan and classical learning (via the Arabs and Byzantium) helped to stimulate the arts and sciences under the patronage of popes and princes in Italy and elsewhere. This became known as the Renaissance (meaning rebirth) and its leading figures – Leonardo, Michelangelo, Raphael – have become household names.

Reactions against corruption in the Church in Germany at this time led by a fiery Augustinian monk called Martin Luther resulted in another Europe-wide cultural movement that was destined to be every bit as influential as the Renaissance on the development of modernity. The Reformation divided Christians in the West. While the Catholic Church set about reforming itself from within (a process known as the 'Counter-Reformation') the breakaway 'Protestant' or 'Reformed' Churches continued to divide and subdivide, under charismatic figures such as Luther, Calvin and Zwingli. Since one of the characteristics of these movements was a rejection of the authority of the papacy, they lacked a central authority to hold them together. The Bible was their sole authority, interpreted by the leader of the sect or by the individual member of the community. One of the strengths of the reform movement, however, was the perception that ordinary people needed to be able to hear and read the Scriptures for themselves. The new technology of printing would eventually make it possible for there to be a Bible in every home.

It should be noted that one of the forces driving the Reformation was hardly religious at all. It was the political and economic rise of the local warlords and monarchs, who perceived an advantage to themselves in separation from both pope and emperor. European Christendom began to fragment into a mosaic of nation states, in which the prevailing religious loyalty was determined by the king rather than tradition. Theological differences and the emotional antipathy to corrupt priests and popes provided a convenient excuse to assert a rival authority.

Politics played a role in the English Reformation. King Henry VIII, though theologically conservative, decided to break with Rome after failing to get an annulment to end his first marriage. This resulted immediately in the seizure of monastic lands and property by Henry's henchmen, and the destruction of monastic life in England. After his death, the country remained in a perpetual see-saw of religious affiliation, which cost many lives and created an ever more savage backlash on all sides. The short-lived Edward VI favoured hard-line Protestant reform, while in Mary's reign some of the Protestant leaders were executed for heresy. Elizabeth I wanted to pursue a middle way, but in practice, from this point on the politics of the country set the split from Rome in stone. A papal bull in 1570, excommunicating Elizabeth for not returning to the practice of the Catholic faith, implicated English Catholics as potential sources of treason. Not only priests such as the Jesuit St Edmund Campion, but also courageous lay people such as St Margaret Clitherow were hounded, tortured and killed for simply practising the Catholic faith. This situation continued for several hundred years. Until the repeal of the penal laws in the eighteenth century, Catholics couldn't go to university or stand for political office.

Throughout Europe, in countries where the Reformation took hold, the idea that a king could determine the religious beliefs of his subjects became increasingly hard to sustain. The doctrine that each person must be permitted to interpret the Bible for himself, which led to the availability of new vernacular translations and wider literacy, went hand in hand with a new emphasis on private conscience. Catholics also believe in conscience, but not in its isolation from the authority of Church and tradition. After a series of wars between Protestants and Catholics, the scene was set in the seventeenth century for an era of pragmatic toleration, which effectively meant that religion began to be viewed as a private matter of little concern to the state.

The Counter-Reformation

In examining what Catholics believe about history, there is no escaping the unsavoury nature of the Inquisition, a phenomenon that illustrates the uneasy partnership between the triumphalist aspect of the Catholic Church and the body politic. The Inquisition exemplified the tensions that would lead to a new conception of the human individual and human rights.

The Roman Inquisition was established by Paul III in 1542 in response to Protestantism, as a way of centralizing the various episcopal tribunals under the authority of the pope and pushing forward much-needed reforms of the Church. Although it does not suffer from as dark an image as the Spanish Inquisition, the Roman Inquisition has often been criticized for condemning the pantheism of Giordano Bruno (burned at the stake in 1600) and the heliocentric theories of Galileo (condemned to silence in 1632). The earlier Spanish Inquisition was founded by Ferdinand and Isabella of Spain in 1478. It soon began to be used as an instrument of state against both Jews and Muslims – bringing to an end any peaceful coexistence (*convivencia*) of Christianity, Judaism and Islam – and especially against those who converted to Christianity but were suspected of secretly maintaining their previous beliefs.

The Spanish Inquisition differed from the medieval and Roman Inquisitions in that it was primarily an agency of the Crown rather than the Church, which partly explains its harsher methods. Nevertheless, the popular caricatures may not be completely accurate. Though torture was permitted as a way of extracting confessions, conditions in its prisons were still fairly good by the standard of the times and there is even evidence that some prisoners in secular prisons deliberately made blasphemous remarks or announced they were heretics in order to be transferred to the care of the Spanish Inquisition.

Despite the Inquisition, Spain produced several great saints who helped to inspire a Catholic Reformation whose influence was felt around the world. St Ignatius of Loyola (whose *Spiritual Exercises* was at first included on the Inquisition's Index of censored books) founded a religious order called the Society of Jesus, and these Jesuits played a key role in Catholic intellectual and spiritual renewal, providing countless missionaries and martyrs, from England to Paraguay to Japan. The Counter-Reformation period was dominated by the Jesuits in the way the Franciscan and Dominican friars had dominated a previous age, and is associated with the great artistic movement of the baroque. The other main source of this Catholic cultural movement is, of course, Italy, which produced its own great saints, figures like Charles Borromeo and Philip Neri, many of whose disciples are numbered among the popes of the time.

The Carmelites had developed earlier, in the twelfth century, as a community living on Mount Carmel in the Holy Land, in imitation of the ancient prophet Elijah. By the time of the Counter-Reformation the order had become somewhat corrupt. The woman who struggled to reform them in the sixteenth century, Teresa of Avila, also came under threat from the Inquisition. Yet she is now recognized as a saint and a Doctor of the Church (i.e. someone of exemplary orthodoxy) along with her ally St John of the Cross, and their mystical teachings are among the treasures of the Church. In the modern era these bloomed anew in another great Carmelite saint and doctor: St Theresa of Lisieux (d. 1897), whose enormously influential autobiography *Story of a Soul* taught people a way to seek holiness in ordinary everyday life.

Into the Modern Era

The split between northern European Reformation culture and the Catholic Renaissance had far-reaching effects. In England, particularly, the flowering of Christian humanism, which had begun as a Catholic movement fostered by St Thomas More in dialogue with figures such as Erasmus, evolved into something more secular. England became a powerhouse of trade and industry, and a leader in the scientific revolution. Meanwhile in Italy and Spain the artistic and cultural splendour of the Renaissance continued to focus on divine things, but now with a more humanistic emphasis. Michelangelo's famous paintings in the Sistine Chapel, while realistic in terms of their depiction of human anatomy, are also laced with symbolic and spiritual meanings. While the extremes of the later baroque style do not appeal to many northern Europeans, it is interesting to speculate whether those extremes derive from a reaction to the mercantile rationalism arising in the north.

Certainly it was the Reformation that prepared the ground for the exaltation of human reason known as the Enlightenment, opposing faith to reason in a way the Middle Ages had not. It provided the natural climate for a new ideal of natural sciences based on empirical study rather than contemplation. Despite the reaction of nineteenth-century Romanticism, with its nostalgia for Gothic culture, it was Rationalism that became intellectually dominant by the twentieth century in previously Protestant countries. By now Europe had broken into a series of separate nation states each claiming the supreme allegiance that the Church had once claimed. If rationalists and revolutionaries thought that the dominance of the Church in the medieval period had been oppressive, new technology provided the tools for a new kind of oppression. As the modern military-industrial complex proliferated, social engineering on a grand scale was needed to feed the economic patterns it established. As a result the (non-religious) wars of the twentieth century have been the most brutal and destructive in history.

For the nineteenth century gave birth to the ideologies of Socialism and Communism, in part as a reaction to the tensions between those who had become rich and powerful through the Industrial Revolution and the trade empires it made possible, and the vast numbers of wage slaves who served them. The Catholic Church reacted with a formulation of social teaching that denounced the injustices of the system but also the dangers of class warfare. The 1891 encyclical (letter) of Pope Leo XIII, *Rerum Novarum* ('Of New Things'), became the inspiration for workers' movements around the world for the next hundred years, but in a sense it was already too late: Communism swept to power in Russia after 1917 and the Fascism that sprang up to oppose it was no better. The world was torn apart by a new kind of 'total' warfare and the twentieth century was a century of blood.

5

'I make all things new': the Church in the world

Then I saw a new heaven and a new earth; for the first heaven and the first earth had passed away, and the sea was no more. And I saw the holy city, new Jerusalem, coming down out of heaven from God, prepared as a bride adorned for her husband; and I heard a loud voice from the throne saying, 'Behold, the dwelling of God is with men. He will dwell with them, and they shall be his people, and God himself will be with them; he will wipe away every tear from their eyes, and death shall be no more, neither shall there be mourning nor crying nor pain any more, for the former things have passed away.' And he who sat upon the throne said, 'Behold I make all things new.'

Revelation 21:1–4

The Catholic Church claims to have a revelation that is relevant to all times, and a teaching that does not essentially change. To affirm those unchanging beliefs we still say the Creeds that were formulated by the early Church. Nevertheless, since part of the teaching is that God engages himself in time through the Incarnation, the Church always has the possibility (within certain limits) of adapting organically to changing circumstances.

Vatican II

The way this happens is partly (and most importantly) through the influence of the saints who appear in every age, to denounce corruption and renew authentic Catholicism as a living force. It is also the responsibility of the bishops, as successors of the Apostles, to ensure that necessary reforms and adaptations are made. At times of crisis bishops are summoned together in an 'ecumenical' council (meaning gathered from all parts of the world) to make decisions together. The most recent of these international Catholic councils was the Second Vatican Council in the 1960s. (The Second completed the work of the First, which took place in 1870 but was interrupted by war.) Vatican II was a 'pastoral' rather than a 'doctrinal' council, called unexpectedly by the elderly Pope John XXIII to address the situation of the Church in the modern world.

(*From the address of Pope John XXIII at the opening of Vatican II in October 1962*)

The salient point of this Council is not, therefore, a discussion of one article or another of the fundamental doctrine of the Church which has repeatedly been taught by the Fathers and by ancient and modern theologians, and which is presumed to be well known and familiar to all.

For this a Council was not necessary. But from the renewed, serene, and tranquil adherence to all the teaching of the Church in its entirety and preciseness, as it still shines forth in the Acts of the Council of Trent and First Vatican Council, the Christian, Catholic, and apostolic spirit of the whole world expects a step forward toward a doctrinal penetration and a formation of consciousness in faithful and perfect conformity to the authentic doctrine, which, however, should be studied and expounded through the methods of research and through the literary forms of modern thought. The substance of the ancient doctrine of the deposit of faith is one thing, and the way in which it is presented is another. And it is the latter that must be taken into great consideration with patience if necessary, everything being measured in the forms and proportions of a magisterium which is predominantly pastoral in character.

In the first half of the twentieth century two developments within the Church prepared the ground for the new Council. One was the so-called 'modernist crisis', provoked by the exaggerated attempt of some theologians to subordinate Catholic teaching to the methods and findings of science and modern philosophy. This denial of the supernatural had been provoked in turn by an earlier, exaggerated separation of nature and grace in the thought of many Church theologians. The second development offered a more balanced way forward for the Church, integrating the concern for orthodoxy and tradition with a respect for modern scholarship. Known as the *Ressourcement*, or 'return to sources', it sought renewal by looking back to the documents and practice of the early Church. Men such as

Henri de Lubac SJ, Yves Congar, Louis Bouyer and Hans Urs von Balthasar led a revival of biblical scholarship and encouraged modest liturgical reform.

It was arguably this movement that did most to shape the Second Vatican Council, although changes in the liturgy caused many upheavals. Not only was the Mass now said in the vernacular, but its very form was altered. Having Mass in the vernacular has had a beneficial impact on the comprehension and spiritual participation of the faithful. Yet in the enthusiasm for new experiments, the sacred and contemplative nature of the Mass was all too often forgotten.

The present pope, Benedict XVI, who has an abiding interest in the liturgy and has written extensively on the subject, has for some years been involved in a movement to restore beauty and the symbolic dimension in all the existing rites, including the English translation, which is presently undergoing revision. He has also promoted the revival of the older 'Tridentine' rite, believing that its active use can help improve the newer rite. It is commonly thought that the Latin Mass has been abolished since Vatican II. This is not the case: the new rite was originally promulgated in Latin and this form is still used at High Masses all over the world. And as I said, the old Latin rite is increasingly available for those who wish to attend it.

Perhaps the most important contribution of the council, apart from its more irenic and charitable pastoral style, and the thawing of relations with Protestants and Orthodox, was the adoption of a new philosophical approach known as 'personalism'. This involved no change in doctrine, but it applied existing doctrine about Christ to many of the distinctive problems of modern culture (such as a pervasive feeling of 'alienation'). The new approach was due in part to the influence

of a philosopher-bishop from Poland, who was one of the
Council Fathers and later became Pope John Paul II. It gave a
new and impressive emphasis to human freedom and conscience, while seeing human beings as existing primarily not as
'individuals' (and therefore always tending to be isolated and
competitive) but as 'persons' (existing in relationships of mutual
dependence and cooperation).

This new 'personalist' approach entailed recognizing that
what the Gospels tell us about Christ actually reveals as much
about man as it does about God, as we saw in chapter 1: 'The
truth is that only in the mystery of the incarnate Word does the
mystery of man take on light. For Adam, the first man, was a
figure of him who was to come, namely Christ the Lord. Christ,
the final Adam, by the revelation of the mystery of the Father
and his love, fully reveals man to man himself and makes his
supreme calling clear' (*Gaudium et Spes*, 22). About God, it
reveals that the divine nature is love. About man, it reveals that
our only human fulfilment is precisely the same self-giving love
that we see in Christ: man can 'fully discover his true self only
in a sincere giving of himself' (section 24). All through his long
pontificate, John Paul II tried to apply these insights to the
numerous situations he had to face. And his successor, Benedict
XVI, devoted his first encyclical (major teaching document) to
the same task.

Deus Caritas Est ('God Is Love') by Pope Benedict is an
eloquent and easy-to-read synthesis of this important new
direction in Catholic thinking, the fruit of the Second Vatican
Council. From it we may move into a consideration of three
key areas where the Church has something important to say to
the modern world: the whole realm of morality, the question
of human sexuality in particular and the conduct of life in
society.

Moral Teaching

When they wrote about morality, John Paul II and Benedict XVI have tended to consider the Gospels on the one hand and the actual human situation on the other. The traditional teaching on natural law, as an objective order of right and wrong inscribed on our hearts by God, is still implicit in these writings. But both men knew that most people today do not think deductively and abstractly. They think more with their feelings and their imagination.

As a result, these recent popes have deliberately moved away from the stress on duty and commandments, in order to show how our moral duties are based on our very nature as human beings. It is our divine calling to happiness with God that energizes our moral life. We are called not just to be well behaved, but to be deeply transformed with the help of grace into a new creature, a saint. Vatican II talked of a 'universal vocation to holiness' and, while this may seem daunting, it is also consoling, because we know that God will not leave us alone in this struggle. Without him such a thing would be impossible; but with him even ordinary people, damaged people, can become sanctified.

The ultimate point of the moral life is to be happy. Catholics are accused of thinking that happiness must always lead to darkness, or that grim stoicism and inner misery are signs of holiness. There are Catholics like this: they are in fact sliding into the heresy of Jansenism, which dwells obsessively on the unworthiness of the human person to participate in the divine life, to the point where the subject loses contact with the sense of God's love. The Catholic Church actually teaches that one of the most important signs of holiness is joy.

Deep down we all know that the only way to become happy

is to love and to be loved. Catholic moral teaching is based around this same truth. St Thomas Aquinas, one of Catholicism's greatest moral philosophers, put it in this way: he said that love is the 'form' of the virtues, meaning that love is the pattern and source of all that makes a person good and admirable. Love is like white light, while the various virtues (courage, kindness, faithfulness, generosity, honesty, etc.) are like the individual colours that make it up when blended together.

As Pope Benedict has put it, God commands us to love our neighbour (Mark 12:29–31). Jesus through his parables makes us understand that our 'neighbour' is not just our kinsman, but absolutely anyone who needs our help. God can only *command* us to love because he has first given us love himself, by giving himself to us on the Cross. We learn how to love not as a theoretical exercise or a feeling, a sentiment, but because we experience ourselves as loved by that Other. It is an engagement with reality, and that reality connects myself, the other person and God, who is the basis of the link between human beings. We all have our origin and end in him, and he is more deeply present to me than I am to myself (as Pope Benedict writes in *Deus Caritas Est*, section 17, quoting St Augustine).

Theology of the Body

Talk of love can sound very vague. Everyone claims to love and the most terrible crimes have been excused in its name. In his encyclical, Pope Benedict explores the nature of love, distinguishing a love that *seeks* (seeks mainly the happiness of the self) from a love that *gives* (for the sake of the other). These he calls *eros* and *agape*. Contrary to some commentators, Pope Benedict emphasizes that we need both dimensions of love and each needs the other, because happiness is only found through self-gift. This is true also on the physical level, for man is not just a soul, any more than he is simply a body. 'Man is truly himself when his body and soul are intimately united; the challenge of *eros* can be said to be truly met when this unification is achieved' (*Deus Caritas Est*, 5).

This could be said to be one of the problems of our age. By separating body and soul, we have been able to turn the body – our own and that of others – into a commodity, a thing to be traded, and sex becomes a pleasure that we seek to acquire and consume, *eros* cut off from *agape*. The growth of pornography and sex slavery in our time, the breakdown of stable marriages and the increase in promiscuity are all, according to the two most recent popes, related to the spread of a dualistic and consumerist mentality. We become alienated from our own bodies, in the sense that we regard them not as a part of ourselves – our physical dimension – but as our 'property'. If I own something, I am separate from it. If I am merely the 'owner' of my body I can hate it or love it, rebuild or replace it, punish or reward it. Furthermore, if I regard other people's bodies also as physical things they happen to possess, I can separate what I do with or to their bodies from any relationship I have with them as persons.

Throughout its history the Catholic Church has been countering dualism with a more integrated view that respects the body as part of the person, that must not be treated as separate. The Gnostics in the early Church thought our destiny was to escape from the world of matter altogether, and for ever, overcoming it through knowledge (*gnosis*). The Manicheans and Cathars in the Middle Ages taught that matter was evil, and the body and marriage to be despised. Yet matrimony is one of the

Church's sacraments because Christ blessed human marriage. This exclusive, faithful and lifelong union of bodies and souls in a covenant of love is created by God as an image of and participation in his own way of loving us. God had joined himself to human flesh and through the resurrection this flesh had entered heaven, opening the way for all of us.

John Paul II developed these teachings further by reflecting not just on the psychology and spirituality of man, and on the teachings of St Paul about marriage (e.g. in the Letter to the Ephesians) but on what was revealed by God in the Book of Genesis. He saw this not as a primitive scientific account of human biological origins (and so not to be set against modern scientific theories of evolution, as though it were an alternative), but as a *theological history*, containing an inspired commentary on the relationship of men and women to each other and to God.

In Pope John Paul's reading, the first chapters of Genesis describe the birth of lust in the human being with the words, 'I was afraid, because I was naked, and I hid myself' (Genesis 3:10). The shame that is the result of eating the forbidden fruit that gives 'knowledge of good and evil' is directly due to the fact that the body is no longer entirely transparent to the spirit, but contains the seeds of a resistance to it. The original unity of body and soul has been ruptured by deliberately going against the voice of conscience, the voice of God in man. A delicate moral 'ecosystem' has been upset and, from then on, the consequences will unfold throughout history, each successive sin making things worse. (It is in order to heal all this that God becomes incarnate as man, the 'second Adam', when the time is ripe.)

For John Paul II the body has a 'nuptial meaning', which is to say that its biological masculinity and femininity is a 'language' through which the calling of man to sincere self-gift can be expressed. Erotic love is subtly but profoundly different from lust. *Eros* serves the 'communion of persons' because it makes the body a gift for the other, whereas lust destroys communion by trying to 'take'. Giving in to lust destroys one's self-mastery and thus the freedom to give oneself to another. The man of lust sees the other's body as something he desires for himself, whereas the man of innocence sees the other's body as invested with the dignity of the other, and loves that body as part of loving the other person as a whole and *as other*.

This respect for the *other* then extends naturally to respect for any child conceived through the union of a man and a woman. Even if the relationship that brought this new life about is a casual or violent one, the life itself is, in Catholic eyes, sacred. The emphasis on the dignity of incarnation means that we cannot contemplate deliberate abortion under any circumstances, however difficult. This can lead to some very delicate medical decisions. A Catholic mother whose life is in danger from pregnancy would be advised not to have an abortion in order to save her own life, but she *would* be permitted to have another kind of operation that might save her life even if it might result in the death of her unborn child. The sin lies in intending to kill one human being in order to save another. If the choice is between one person dying, or two, then a procedure that saves the one person is no sin. It should be added that Pope John Paul II stressed that in what he terms the 'culture of death', women are as much the victims of abortion as their children, since they exist in a society where men, or other family members, often refuse to support fully this most vulnerable of relationships.

Openness to the conception of new life is also closely related to the giving rather than the taking aspect of sex. It is in this context that the famous Catholic ban on artificial methods of birth control (as G. K. Chesterton described it, 'no birth and no control') should be understood. The Church does not oppose the pill and condom because they are artificial, but because they are designed to exclude procreation, which is an intrinsic dimension of the gift of self. Indeed, this procreative aspect safeguards the very mystery of each person. To embrace the other is also to embrace the mystery of the possibility of new life, accepting in love all the challenges that new life will present. This takes us back to the original meaning of the word *eros* – the prolongation, deepening and broadening of desire for the beloved; for what better prolongs the beloved in time and thus desire for the beloved than a new human life? The result, then, of contraception is to undermine the element of true *eros* in the relationship.

The ban on artificial contraception has put the Church at odds with those who want to promote the use of condoms against HIV infection. This particular matter is still being discussed in detail by theologians, but the official Catholic line seems to be that making condoms available will only encourage the continuation of the behaviour that led to the problem in the first place. The most effective way of preventing the spread of infection is by encouraging abstinence from sex outside marriage, even if this is a hard thing to say in a culture that believes that people cannot live for long without sex.

There is no space here to go into the more detailed arguments around this subject, but suffice it to say that the development of natural fertility awareness, with improved techniques for predicting the intricacies of the female cycle, do seem to some extent to vindicate the stance of *Humanae Vitae* (1968). This encyclical of Pope Paul VI's is associated with the controversial ban on artificial contraception. It certainly pitched itself headlong against the cultural ethos of its time, at least in the developed countries of the world. Intended to stand for the primacy of unconditional love, *Humanae Vitae* remains a sign of contradiction between the Church and the world.

Social Teaching

The Catholic Church has always had a doctrine about society; that is to say, teachings that in one way or another apply to politics, economics, crime and punishment, family, war and living in community. The earliest Christians shared all their possessions, and supported one another through the darkest times of persecution and poverty. Later, when Christianity became the established religion, many still showed their faith by lives of integrity, service to others, charity to the poor and faithfulness in marriage. Others renounced the lure of a comfortable life in the cities, and withdrew to the wilderness to create the first monastic settlements, 'communes' where rules of behaviour and common work were devised that protected oases of civilized life during the barbarian invasions.

The struggle to apply the Christian principle of 'love your neighbour' took many forms and the principle led to many social experiments, some more successful than others. Slavery was acceptable in the Roman Empire, but after a few centuries of Christian influence it had begun to disappear. War was never outlawed – indeed, it remained fierce and bloody – but attempts were made to control, limit and reduce it, as we have seen. Priests were not allowed to shed blood and laypeople who joined the Franciscan movement were also forbidden to bear arms. By the late Middle Ages a vast network of monasteries protected the poor and harboured the sick, to such an extent that when they were suddenly abolished in England a new class of dispossessed was created and Poor Laws were passed to offer some refuge. In the Middle Ages, also, a system of 'guilds' supported workers in the various crafts and trades. These effectively served to provide training, guarantee quality control, insure against illness and bereavement, and give a religious pattern and foundation to working life.

These and other manifestations of Catholic faith helped to shape and humanize society in Europe, but it was not until the collapse of aristocratic rule, the formation of the modern industrial state and the rise of Communism in the nineteenth century that the Church started to formulate the coherent body of teachings known today as 'Catholic Social Doctrine'. As mentioned before, Pope Leo XIII wrote an encyclical in 1891 called *Rerum Novarum*, which laid the groundwork. The conflict between capital and labour created a new situation, and required society to be structured in a new way to ensure justice.

Pope Leo made a point of supporting workers' rights, but condemned the concept of inevitable class warfare. He encouraged cooperation through trades unions, argued that employers must provide a living wage and stressed the importance to society of protecting the family. During the hundred years that followed other popes took up the baton, responding to the changing circumstances of the twentieth century, with the rise of Fascism and consumerism. In Latin America and Africa, the 1960s and 1970s saw the rise of a theological movement known as 'Liberation Theology', based on the attempt to make the poor more conscious of their oppression through meditation on the Bible in local 'base communities'. The movement was discouraged by the Vatican in the belief that it fostered class conflict and was partly driven by an ideological reading of Scripture.

In Europe and elsewhere, Communism fell in 1989. Pope John Paul II (Karol Wojtyla) had been involved with political initiatives in his native Poland throughout the Second World War and into the Communist era. He formed part of the underground movement against the Nazis, by helping to smuggle food and drugs into the Warsaw ghetto, and keeping Polish cultural initiatives going (the Germans had banned Polish theatre, for instance). When the Communists moved in after the war, Wojtyla began to assist working-class resistance to the new regime, fostering the Solidarity movement, which eventually helped to topple Communist power. As pope, he made it his business in *Centesimus Annus* to summarize the complex body of Catholic social doctrine sparked off in Pope Leo's encyclical a century before. A *Compendium of Social Doctrine* was later published that consolidates all this work, including the more recent developments emphasizing the importance of care for the environment.

These are the key points of Catholic social teaching:

1 **Dignity of the Human Person** This is the foundation of the rest. Made in the image of God, man is not just a material body but a person, with an inviolable conscience, existing in relationship to others, mutually dependent. Whatever their differences, men and women, and people of every race and age, size, creed and colour, are of equal dignity. The value of a person does not depend on appearance or ability. The only proper response to the dignity of each human person is love.

2 **Charity, Common Good and Community** Thus we form one human family, and the good for man is not just an individual good but a common good in which the individual good participates. Human beings must try

therefore to work together to ensure the common good in political and economic life.

3 Family as the Basic Cell of Society The most fundamental form of human society is the family, founded on the union of a man and a woman in the task of generating and educating children.

4 Justice: Rights and Responsibilities Personal dignity is codified in the form of 'rights', but every right is the flip side of a responsibility or duty. The first of rights is a right to life, whose flip side is the duty of others to protect, nourish and support human life from its beginning to its natural end. Rights to spiritual goods have priority over rights to material ones.

5 Government and Subsidiarity The state should serve the person and the family rather than itself, or the Head of State, so economic and political decisions must be made at the lowest level possible, rather than from the top down. In order to promote the dignity and freedom of each person, power should be distributed or devolved rather than centralized, through local government, regionalism, educational empowerment and economic cooperation.

6 Economic Justice The earth and its goods are intended for everyone, but these goods are not static, they grow depending on the work man puts into them. As part of his dignity, man has a right to own certain things for himself, and also to the fruits of his labour, and he also has a right to labour, to work itself. Those in need also have a right to a share in those fruits, so the needs of others must in certain circumstances take priority over private ownership.

7 Preferential Option for the Poor Again, since human

beings should serve each other, priority should be given not to the self (or those most immediately connected with us) but to the other, and first of all to those who have the greatest need, whoever they may be, through freely given charity and also through the proper ordering of society.

8 Stewardship of God's Creation   The whole natural world is a 'common good' for all generations, a gift to man whose role is not to exploit and destroy it but to protect and enable it to flourish sustainably, even while drawing upon it to support his own existence. Our fellow creatures must be treated with kindness.

9 Global Solidarity and Development   If these principles are applied worldwide, we see that there is a *global* common good, not just a national one. The principles of justice apply to peoples and nations and to the relationship between different parts of the world. Economic development in one place should not be at the cost of poverty and deprivation in another.

10 Promotion of Peace and Disarmament   Pope John Paul II said that, 'Peace is not just the absence of war. It involves mutual respect and confidence between peoples and nations. It involves collaboration and binding agreements.' Peace is the fruit of justice and is dependent upon right order among human beings. With modern technology, war is too dangerous to be used as an instrument of policy, although proportionate self-defence is always legitimate.

Catholic teaching about society is complex but also balanced and flexible. It is based on some fundamental principles, and also on centuries of historical experience under many different regimes and economic systems. It enables criticism both of Socialist and of capitalist economic systems, because it speaks both of the right to property and yet also of social responsibility and the common good. It is opposed to consumerism, in the sense of a system where we exist and work in order to consume, and measure our worth by what we possess and our freedom by the number of choices we have in the supermarket.

Epilogue

The Conversation

On the third day there was a wedding at Cana in Galilee, and the mother of Jesus was there; Jesus also was invited to the marriage, with his disciples. When the wine failed, the mother of Jesus said to him, 'They have no wine.' And Jesus said to her, 'O woman, what have you to do with me? My hour has not yet come.' His mother said to the servants, 'Do whatever he tells you.' Now six stone jars were standing there, for the Jewish rites of purification, each holding twenty or thirty gallons. Jesus said to them, 'Fill the jars with water.' And they filled them up to the brim. He said to them, 'Now draw some out, and take it to the steward of the feast.' So they took it. When the steward of the feast tasted the water now become wine, and did not know where it came from (though the servants who had drawn the water knew), the steward of the feast called the bridegroom and said to him, 'Every man serves the good wine first; and when men have drunk freely, then the poor wine; but you have kept the good wine until now.' This, the first of his signs, Jesus did at Cana in Galilee, and manifested his glory; and his disciples believed in him.

John 2:1–11

I have talked about St Peter as the 'head' of the body that is the Church. Now I must come to who, or what, constitutes the *heart*. For this we have to go back to the actual historical heart beating over the body of the Christ child during the nine months of his gestation in a human womb. While the Church appears to be a very patriarchical institution if you look at the preponderance of men running it, she is also bound up with a profoundly feminine mystery.

There are two ways for love to express itself – one has been dealt with when we looked at the passion of Christ: 'Greater love hath no man than to lay down his life for his friends.' Suffering is an inevitable consequence of love in a world where people are sundered from one another by sin. But there would be no point to suffering if it were not done for the sake of love. Which is why the mother's heart is pierced through when she sees the son she loves being rejected and tortured. She suffers with him and so do all Christians who come after her.

The other manifestation of love is expressed through feeding. The first thing a mother does for her child is feed him. She feeds him from her own body. In the womb, the child participates in the body of the mother, receives his food from her without her even thinking about it. Once born he receives nourishment from her through a conscious yet instinctive process. She sets about nurturing her child, because that is what the child needs.

Food will always be a crucial expression of love. People unite round a table to share food. In doing so, they not only share physical nourishment, but also something more subtle, something ineffable. They share in one another's lives. In the film *Babette's Feast*, to express her gratitude to the people who have sheltered her in time of trouble, Babette sets about creating a feast. A feast is an expression of something that goes way beyond the bare necessities, that expresses *to the full* the generosity of the woman's heart, the desire of the giver to pour herself out for her guests. She spends every last penny she has to procure the feast. It is a culinary tour de force, a work of art. And it brings about a transformation in those who receive it. Taking their time to share the meal, to be fully *present* to one another, they become open to grace, open to something beyond the everyday. They forget their problems, their arguments, their limited perception of what life has to offer. They become enchanted by the gift, lifted out of time.

This is why Jesus chooses a meal, takes food, to convey himself fully to his followers, not just in the Last Supper, but in perpetuity, through time immemorial. In uniting himself with us under the form of physical nourishment – the things we cannot do without, our daily bread – he anchors the interior meaning of the gift in the one thing that unites us all, that signifies the possibility of existence.

What Is This to You and Me?

But he not only chooses bread. He also chooses wine. Wine is not strictly speaking a necessity. Yet Jesus allies it with the bread and makes it a necessary part of his gift. Why? Would water not have done just as well, or better?

The clue to this choice lies in the very first recorded miracle of Christ's life in John's Gospel: the wedding at Cana. This is in fact the only record of a direct conversation between Jesus and his Mother. It contains within it the mystical core of Christianity, the pattern whereby Christians find themselves invited to imitate Mary in our relations with her Son. In this passage the meaning of prayer is conveyed. They are both at a wedding, at Cana in Galilee. It seems that there are too many guests, or perhaps the guests are particularly thirsty, so the wine runs out. Mary points this out to her Son. Here Mary demonstrates the truest kind of intercessory prayer. She doesn't say, 'Please do such and such about the situation.' She merely draws his attention to it. She, who was always in the presence of God, feels the need to offer the problem to him. She as it were unites her *attention* with his.

The response that he gives his Mother seems on the surface of it like a rebuke, almost as though Jesus were impatient, even irritable with her. 'O woman,' he says, 'what have you to do with me? My hour has not yet come.' Curious response! What can it mean? Yet it relates directly to the passion and death of Jesus. Because at this point he has not yet set out on his public ministry – that chain of events which will lead, inexorably, to his arrest and death.

'Woman' he calls her. The Hebrew rendering of the passage, a Jewish friend tells me, should read something like: 'Woman: what is this to you and me?' Translate the first word as 'Lady' and the effect is very different. In one way a rebuke might be expected, for indeed she seems to have hinted that he can, and should, intervene in the natural course of events. By doing this she has in some sense given the game away. She is revealing his secret identity. If this were an ordinary mother-son relationship, we might well conclude that he was annoyed. But it is not and Mary's response to the seeming rebuke proves it. Calmly she turns to the servants and tells them, 'Do whatever he tells you.' And Jesus, far from ignoring his Mother's plea on behalf of the wedding party, turns not just one jar, but many jars – large jars containing many gallons of water – into wine. And not just any old wine, the 'best wine'.

The Holy Grail

Jesus does not create wine out of nowhere. He uses something that is already there: water. He takes the basic necessity, the substance without which life on the planet is not possible, and transforms it. It becomes another substance, a substance that not only quenches thirst, but also expresses the superabundance of life experienced in community. Wine is a social necessity at a Jewish feast. A wedding without wine, in that context, is unthinkable. This is why the lack of wine is such a bad sign, a source of shame that Mary wants to spare her friends.

We often lack what we ought to have thought of providing. We are limited creatures, with limited time, limited resources, limited attention. But God, physically present in our midst as the man Jesus, wants to care for us body and soul, and he provides for us from his limitless store. He takes our bare necessity and turns it into something that expresses his generosity, his superabundance.

However, he does not do this in a vacuum, any more than he makes the wine from nothing. It seems that at first he may not want to do it at all. He only acts in response to a human initiative. Herein lies the tremendous mystery of love between God and us, the dialogue between the human soul and the divine will. The wedding at Cana is the first recorded example of Christian intercessory prayer and the first hint at the Eucharistic core of the faith, that reality which for Catholics anchors their prayer life in the contemplation of Christ's ultimate gift.

The wedding at Cana also confirms the profoundly nuptial nature of the Christian revelation, that I and Thou discourse between man and woman, God and the human person. It has all the qualities of a formal enactment, almost a ritual, concerning what Mary knows about her Son. He treats her now, not as his Mother, but as the Woman representing all women, Eve to his Adam. Here at Cana, Mary becomes a new 'mother of all the living' (Genesis 3:20) appealing to God for the things we need. 'And his disciples believed in him.' By pointing out what is needed, and then turning in confidence to her fellow human beings and asking them to cooperate with him, she becomes the very embodiment of faith. She is, from the start, as the Church describes her, Mother of disciples, Queen of Apostles.

The water, soon to become a symbol of grace as well as cleansing, turns into something else, into the wine later to be associated with Christ's own blood. Blood is what he shares with the woman who bore him into the world, and that blood will be shed by a world that does not recognize him: 'Take this, all of you, and drink from it, this is the cup of my blood, the blood of the new and everlasting covenant. It will be shed for all, so that sins may be forgiven.'

There is such a thing as the bloodline of Christ, but it has not been perpetuated through some elite family tree. It has been made available to all, under the guise of the simplest things possible: bread and wine, becoming the Real Presence of God in the Eucharistic feast.

Further reading

Official Church Documents

Catechism of the Catholic Church: Popular and Definitive Edition (London: Burns & Oates)
[For online versions see *www.scborromeo.org/ccc/ccc_toc2.htm* and also *www.nccbuscc.org/catechism/*]
Compendium of the Catechism (London: CTS)
[Online from *www.vatican.va/archive/compendium_ccc/documents/ archive_2005_compendium-ccc_en.html*]
Compendium of the Social Doctrine of the Church (London: Continuum)
[*www.vatican.va/roman_curia/pontifical_councils/justpeace/docu ments/rc_pc_justpeace_doc_20060526_compendio-dott-soc_en.html*]
Gaudium et Spes and other documents of Vatican II (available from CTS)
[*www.stjosef.at/council/*]
Pope Benedict XVI, *Deus Caritas Est* (London: CTS)
Pope John Paul II, *Mulieris Dignitatem* (London: CTS)
[Along with all other papal encyclicals, online from *www.vatican.va/ holy_father*]

Other Books

Balthasar, H.U. von, *Credo: Meditations on the Apostles' Creed* (San Francisco: Ignatius Press)

Beckett, Lucy, *In the Light of Christ: Writings in the Western Tradition* (San Francisco: Ignatius Press). This is a highly readable overview of the major writers who have had a bearing on the interaction between Christian faith and culture.

Caldecott, Stratford, *The Seven Sacraments: Entering the Mysteries of God* (San Francisco: Crossroad)

Holden, Marcus and Andrew Pinsent, *Credo: The Catholic Faith Explained* (London: CTS)

Kreeft, Peter, *Catholic Christianity* (San Francisco: Ignatius Press)

McCoy, Alban, *An Intelligent Person's Guide to Catholicism* (London: Continuum)

These last two books are more challenging to read, but are included as they are seminal books on crucial aspects of modern Catholic thinking, for those who are interested.

Lubac, Henri de, *Catholicism: Christ and the Common Destiny of Man* (San Francisco: Ignatius Press)

Newman, John Henry, *An Essay on the Development of Christian Doctrine* (London: Longmans, Greene & Co.)

Websites

The Catholic Encyclopaedia: *www.newadvent.org/cathen*
CTS (Catholic Truth Society): *www.cts-online.org.uk*
The Holy See: www.vatican.va
Universalis Catholic Calendar: *www.universalis.com*

Glossary

altar – the table of sacrifice on which the consecration and offering of the Eucharist takes place.

angels – literally 'messengers' (of God): created but non-material intelligences capable of appearing to human beings but not normally embodied in space or time.

apologetics – the art of explaining or presenting the Catholic faith (not to be confused with the art of making apologies). One who does this is called an 'apologist'.

Apostle – literally 'person sent': one of the twelve disciples of Jesus specially chosen to go out and preach the Gospel and heal the sick (e.g. Mark 6:7–13).

apostolate – the particular task or mission of an Apostle.

apostolic succession – the passing on of the authority and mission of the twelve Apostles to their successors, the bishops.

ascension – the 'going up' to heaven of the body of the resurrected Christ as described in Mark 16:19, Luke 24:51 and Acts 1:9.

assumption – the 'taking up' of the body of the Virgin Mary at the end of her earthly life into heaven.

Blessed Sacrament, see **Eucharist**.

Blessed Virgin Mary, see **Mary**.

canon (of Scripture) – a way of referring to the selection of books that have been accepted as part of Holy Scripture.

canonization – the procedure by which a person, once dead, is pronounced by the authorities of the Church to be in heaven with God, able to hear the prayers of the faithful and capable of **intercession** (qv) with God.

catechism – a summary of the Catholic faith, either official (*The Catechism of the Catholic Church*) or unofficial. Catechesis is the process whereby someone is instructed in the faith.

catechumen – a person undergoing instruction in the Catholic faith probably with a view to reception into the Church.

Catholic – literally 'universal', in the sense of being found the world over or enfolding the world, used to refer especially to things, practices and people belonging to the Roman Catholic Church, but also applied by some to Christians not in communion with the pope who nevertheless share most of their beliefs with the Roman Catholics (for example a branch of the Anglican Church called the Anglo-Catholics).

Christendom – a transnational political realm where Christian faith is generally accepted as the norm, or more specifically the medieval European domain in which the rulers of the various states owed allegiance to the pope.

communion – a joining together at a deep level, used to refer to the unity that exists in the Church (being 'in communion' with the pope, for example), and by extension to the reception of the Eucharist, sometimes called 'Holy Communion', because this is the sacrament in which Catholics are joined together and become a Church.

consecration – the act whereby something or someone is specifically given over to the service of God, such as priests or people in religious orders and communities. Also refers to the part of the Mass when the host becomes the Body of Christ.

covenant – or testament: a profound union of persons based on a mutual undertaking of fidelity to an agreement. The Jews called themselves the 'People of the Covenant' since God had chosen them for a special relationship with him. The Christians refer to the 'New Covenant' made by Jesus Christ at the **Last Supper** (qv).

creed – any set of beliefs, or more specifically a short summary of the Christian faith approved by the early Church; e.g. the Apostles' Creed, the Nicene Creed (which is always recited at Mass on Sundays), the Athanasian Creed.

crusade – literally 'marked by the Cross': refers primarily to a military campaign conducted in the name of the Church between 1095 and 1291 to recapture for **Christendom** (qv) lands overrun by the Muslims, including **the Holy Land** (qv) and parts of Spain.

dogma – a belief or doctrine held by Catholics to be taught authoritatively by the Church as an intrinsic part of Catholic belief.

Easter – the Christian festival of the death and Resurrection of Jesus Christ, the 'paschal mysteries' at the centre of the Church year, including the 'Triduum' (three days) of Good Friday, Holy Saturday and Easter Sunday. Always takes place in the spring, but dates vary depending on the cycle of the moon.

ecclesiastical – pertaining to the *ekklesia* (originally 'gathering') or community of the faithful, i.e. the Church.

encyclical – an official circular letter from the pope sent to his fellow bishops and others, used as an instrument of official teaching (see **magisterium**).

Eucharist – the sacrament, also known as Holy Communion, in which bread and wine are consecrated and offered to God the Father by a Catholic priest representing Christ during the ceremony of the Mass. After the consecration the bread and wine are deemed no longer to exist as such but have become the Real Presence of Jesus Christ himself. See also **Transubstantiation**.

evangelist – someone who evangelizes, or more specifically one of the four authors of the Gospels in the New Testament of the Bible, who either knew Jesus or were basing themselves on eyewitness accounts of his life and teachings.

faith – one of three 'theological virtues' along with hope and love. The power of the soul to trust in a revelation of God.

Fall, the – the process described (albeit in somewhat mythological terms) in the third chapter of the Book of Genesis by which the first human beings deliberately disobeyed God and were as a result, along with their descendants, deprived of their original state of innocence and grace.

Father, God the – the first divine Person of the Holy Trinity (see **Trinity, Holy**), defined as the origin of the other two (the Son and the Holy Spirit).

fundamentalist – commonly used to mean someone who interprets the Scriptures literally, without taking account of the different genres and spiritual meaning of the texts.

Good Friday – one of the three holy days of Easter, the day commemorating Christ's death on the Cross, through which humanity was freed from the power of evil.

Gospel – the 'good news' of Jesus Christ; more specifically the term used for each of the first four books of the New Testament, containing eyewitness accounts of the life of Christ.

grace – the help God extends to human beings to enable them to do good and become holy.

Grail, Holy – the legendary cup of the Last Supper that was used to receive drops of Christ's blood from the Cross and became the holiest of relics in Christendom. Associated with the stories of King Arthur and his knights.

heaven – the state of being eternally with God.

hell – the state of being eternally without God.

heresy – a doctrine that is either erroneous or only partially true, according to the **magisterium** (qv) of the Church. The person who clings to such a doctrine is known as a 'heretic'.

hierarchy – the rank or order of offices and roles in the Church, from the pope under Christ at the top, through archbishops and bishops, down to the baptized faithful or 'laity'.

Holy Family, the – the nuclear family of Jesus, Joseph and Mary.

Holy Land, the – the geographical area where Jesus lived, taught and died on earth.

Holy See, the – the 'seat' of Peter and his successors, the popes, situated in Rome.

Holy Spirit, God the – one of the three divine Persons in the Holy Trinity, who manifests himself in the New Testament in the form of a dove or as tongues of fire.

host – a wafer of unleavened bread used in the sacrifice of the Mass.

hypostatic union – the mysterious union of divine and human natures in Jesus Christ.

Immaculate Conception – the unique privilege of the Virgin Mary to have been conceived without any stain of **original sin** (qv).

incarnation – the human body or 'becoming human' of the Son of God.

indulgences – from a word meaning to be kind or tender:

refers to a remission of the temporal punishment due to sin, the guilt of which has been forgiven through confession.

infallibility – in the case of the Church, preservation by God from making a serious error in the promulgation of **dogma** (qv).

Inquisition – the former name of the Congregation for the Doctrine of the Faith, the Church agency for the preservation of sound doctrine and teaching.

intention – the specific desire or wish for which a prayer is offered to God.

intercession – an appeal (in prayer) on behalf of another. The saints in heaven are said to intercede for us at the throne of God.

Last Supper – the Passover meal celebrated by Jesus with his closest disciples on the night before his death.

last things – death, judgement, hell and heaven.

liberation theology – an interpretation of the Scriptures from the point of view of the economically poor and politically oppressed.

litany – a form of rhythmic prayer consisting of invocations of God or the saints according to a variety of titles and symbolic attributes.

liturgy – the formal prayers of the Church performed as a community, such as the Mass.

Lord's Prayer – the prayer taught by Jesus to his disciples beginning 'Our Father, who art in heaven ...'

magisterium – the teaching authority of the Church.

mandorla – the almond-shaped space formed by two arcs often used in sacred art to represent a doorway or window between earth and heaven.

Mary, Blessed Virgin – the Mother of Jesus Christ.

Mass – the Eucharistic celebration of the Catholic Church, instituted by Jesus at the Last Supper, in which his sacrifice on the Cross is made present and the New Covenant renewed.

Miraculous Medal – or Medal of the Immaculate Conception: a small medallion imprinted with an image of the Virgin Mary, various symbols and the words of a prayer revealed by her in an apparition to Saint Catherine Labouré in 1830: *O Mary, conceived without sin, pray for us who have recourse to thee.*

natural law – the moral law of good and evil written on our hearts and known by conscience as well as the teaching of the Church.

original sin – the sin of Adam and Eve by which the original gifts of grace that God had made available to man were lost.

orthodox – 'right thinking': a term used to refer to the Greek and Russian Churches of the East no longer (since around 1054) in full communion with the Roman Catholic Church but whose sacraments are recognized as valid by the latter.

papacy – the office of the pope, the bishop or patriarch of Rome (**the Holy See**), regarded by Catholics as the leader of the world's bishops.

petition, prayer of – a prayer that asks for something.

Pontiff – from 'pontifex' or bridge maker, meaning the pope (see **Papacy**).

purgatory – the state of being purified on the way to heaven.

Real Presence, see **Transubstantiation**.

redemption – literally, 'buying back' or rescuing by the payment of a ransom: applied to the act by which Jesus Christ paid the price of all human sin on our behalf by dying on the Cross, thus earning our freedom.

relics – physical traces or belongings of a canonized saint, regarded as carrying some blessing or grace by virtue of their connection with the saint's life and person.

religious – a 'religious' is a person vowed to the service of God in chastity.

Renaissance – a renewal of culture in the fourteenth to seventeenth centuries, beginning in Italy, and associated with a number of artistic and scientific geniuses such as Leonardo, Michelangelo and Raphael.

Ressourcement – 'return to the sources' for the sake of renewal: refers to a movement in Catholic theology, liturgy and biblical studies in the first half of the twentieth century that prepared the ground for the Second Vatican Council.

rosary – a very popular form of repetitive prayer based on a chain of beads, involving meditation on the mysteries of Christ through the eyes of the Virgin Mary.

sacrament – one of the seven main ritual and symbolic actions of the Catholic Church whereby grace is communicated in the different circumstances of life.

sacramental – a 'sacramental' is anything, such as an image or a prayer or holy water, that helps to convey grace to the human soul.

Scripture – writings that have been accepted by the Church as sacred, true and inspired by God.

Second Vatican Council, see **Vatican II**.

secular – pertaining to this world rather than the spiritual.

sin – an act that deliberately goes against the laws or will of God and the best interests of the human soul.

Son, God the – the second divine Person of the Holy Trinity, of the same divine substance as the Father and Holy Spirit, whose divine nature was joined to the human in Jesus Christ.

theology of the body – an extended series of original theological reflections by Pope John Paul II that opened up new horizons in Catholic thinking about sexuality, gender, marriage and human psychology.

Transubstantiation – the doctrine that the bread and wine consecrated in the Mass become the Body and Blood of Christ, containing the Real Presence of his resurrected Person, that can be received in the form of food.

Trinity, Holy or Blessed – the one God, Creator of the Universe, who is also three Persons, each of whom is equally and completely the same one God while remaining eternally distinct from each other. A doctrine deduced from the teachings and actions of Christ and approved by the early Church councils.

Vatican – the tiny city state where the pope lives and rules.

Vatican II – the Second Vatican Council, an important ecumenical council of the Catholic Church that took place in the early 1960s.

vocation – literally 'calling': the mission given to someone in the Church, or a call to service in a specific 'state of life' such as marriage or the priesthood or religious life as a monk or nun.

Index